Book Synopsis

Being both an anti-Christ society and culture driven has SHIFTED us into waiting on children to form their personalities and exhibit gifts and talents, before we start to explore their identity and affirming their purpose. The result is that we when we speak into their lives, it is rooted in what they do well and not related to what God has said about them. We do not realize that by the time children begin to form a personality, generational curses, patterns, and propensities have already taken root in their DNA. Counterfeit identity, personality, soul, bloodline, and familiar spirits have begun to influence their character, nature, and desires. The purpose of this book is to teach the importance of cultivating destiny from the womb so that your child grows up in the ordained purpose of God.

Cultivating Destiny from the Womb

Contact Taquetta Baker
Kingdomshifterscec@gmail.com
(Website) Kingdomshifters.com
Connect with Taquetta via Facebook or YouTube

Contact Shannon White
(Website) Kingdomconvos.org
(Website) Theshannonwhite.com
Connect with Shannon via Facebook

Contact Brandy Reese
Connect with Brandy via Facebook

Table of Contents

Taquetta's Bio

Taquetta has 18 godchildren. She also has six young adult children that she mentors in their personal destiny and calling. Each of them has either a business, ministry, or organization that they personally founded with her assistance. She helped them seek out God's plan for their lives versus secular ambitions and striving to live a partially fulfilled life through the world's system. Though Taquetta ministers to the masses, she is called to the millennials and to the younger generations. Taquetta stumbled upon destiny in her 30's and believes that if she had known her destiny at a young age, she would have not had to play catch up. Her passion is to make sure that others know God at a young age, examine their purpose, learn and cultivate a lifestyle of destiny. The achievement is to work God's plan until we live a fulfilled life that reflects purity and accomplishment. Taquetta ministers, counsels, and mentors through the wells of warfare and worship. She carries an apostolic mantle of judging and establishing God's kingdom in individuals, families, ministries, communities, and regions. Taquetta travels in foreign missions and throughout the United States. She has mentored and established dance and prophetic ministries. At every level of ministry, she claims miracles, signs, and wonders. Taquetta ministers in the areas of fine arts, prayer, fivefold ministry, deliverance, healing, miracles, atmospheric worship. She radiates empowerment by mentoring people in their destiny.

Taquetta's Credentials

- Founder. Kingdom Shifters Ministries (KSM), Indiana & Kingdom Shifters Empowerment Church, Virginia
- Founder, Kingdom Wellness Counseling and Mentoring Center
- Author of over 38 books and 2 prayer decree CD's
- Doctorate in Ministry from Rapha Deliverance University
- Master's Degree in Community Counseling with an emphasis on Marriage, Children and Family Counseling
- Bachelor's Degree in Psychology
- Associates Degree in Business Administration
- Therapon Belief Therapist Certification from the Therapon Institute (faith-based counseling)
- Board of Directors for New Day Community Ministries, Inc.
- Graduate of Eagles Dance Institute under Dr. Pamela Hardy; licensed in the area of liturgical dance
- Apostolic Ordination by Bishop Jackie Green, Founder of JGM-National Prayer Life Institute (Phoenix, AZ)
- Previous ministry service as prophet, visionary for Shekinah Expressions Dance Troupe, teacher, member of presbytery, overseer for altar workers' ministry
- Overseer of Be Thou Made Whole Ministry, Manifold Grace Ministry, and outreach ministry for Ball State University students.

Shannon's Bio

Shannon White is on a mission to ensure parents (especially mothers) train their children to experience God daily, NOT just at church! She believes kids are never too young to know WHO they are in Christ, and that it is up to the parents to teach them WHOSE they are early, so society and social media does not become their means of validation. Shannon is a lover of Jesus, wife, mother of two, professional school counselor, mentor, author, speaker and founder of Kingdom Convos LLC. She specializes in training mothers with children in Kindergarten through high school to develop their children's gifts and talents. The ultimate purpose is to build God confidence and identity in children, such that they walk in God's distinct image of themselves at a young age, thus avoiding being victims to the peer pressures of the world. She teaches women to see their child through God's eyes and the destiny he envisions for their life. Parents can recognize, develop, and cultivate their child in their spiritual gifts and callings, while being able to provide biblical guidance that is age appropriate and applicable to the present time as well as the future. Because of Shannon, mothers see their child experience God in a divinely ordained way! Her goal is to show mothers not just the "how to" of parenting but transforming them into spiritual trainers so their child can be a champion of God's way and NOT the ways the world would project onto them. Shannon White is a transformative leader in empowering generations through training parents, particularly mothers. She is an essential dynamic in our chaotic world!

Brandie's Bio

Brandie Reese is a perfect example of a woman who has a destiny designed by God and held in reserve until she was ready to hear God speak to her about the responsibility of parenting. Her plan for her life and God's ideas for her were on two distinct paths; therefore, her story is one of grace that comes with being equipped. Her journey is a display of the willingness to listen and receive, even when it requires laying aside her own thoughts on what life was going to hold and accepting the journey God had for her.

As a result of her surrender, Brandie has a heart to see families restored and whole. She is passionate about the coming generation and leaving a legacy of contending for the faith. As the mother of two daughters, twin boys, and two stepdaughters, she is on the front line of functioning as a spiritual visionary for blended families. She and her husband embrace their responsibilities to guide and nurture their children in kingdom values. The two of them are miracle parents as Brandie never imagined having children, and when the pregnancies came, health complications put mother and child at risk.

Brandie's passion is to share the truth of God to others, and she walks in that vision in her ministry and her career. She is an ordained minister and certified counselor. Brandie has a Bachelor's in Criminal Justice and Criminology, and a Master's in Cognitive Biblical Therapy. Brandie is a bold soldier in the army of the Lord and is fearless in taking an out-of-the-box stance on parenting, beginning in the womb. Her insights will be a challenge to many readers but be committed to hear the details of her thought process. You will reap the reward of having an open mind and a willing heart.

The Vision of Destiny Unleashed
Dr. Kathy Williams aka Mommak

I am Taquetta's spiritual mother, known as her Mommak. God put us in one another's life when Taquetta was in her mid-20's and finishing her master's degree. She was in a season of consecrating in isolation with God and entering true covenant relationship with with him. While it is a privilege to be an influence on someone with such a powerhouse destiny, it is also a weighty and difficult task. My upbringing is from a small Midwestern town in a traditional family. No one knew how to mentor me when I told people about dreams and my continued statement that, "I just know I am going to see this really happen!" They certainly did not know what to do with all my "why" questions as my thirst for revelation manifested at a very young age. I could read at the age of 3 and have a lifelong passion for learning. My mother told me that when I was 5 years old, I sat with the stock market page fascinated by the numbers. One of the challenges of being revolutionary is that my personality also included rebellion. After spending years at war with everyone around me, God got hold of my life and transformed my energy for the world into a passion for his kingdom. I often wondered what God was thinking to trust me with mentoring and nurturing Taquetta's destiny. It was our mutual love for God, thirst for greater works, and unconditional love of one another that kept us arm-in-arm in the early years. As a Baby Boomer, I often lacked the words or strategy to implement what I knew in my spirit. I often did not know how to guide Taquetta, but she would tell me, "Mommak, I trust that your heart is pure." She moved to Indiana believing that we were to walk in ministry together. God used her heart to position her so that he could then say, "Now, I want to show you why you are here." It has been incredible to watch Taquetta blossom, not only in her own destiny, but in her role of coaching others in their destiny. She IS the spiritual mother to generations. I get the joy of reading books like this one and knowing that parents are being equipped to nurture children who are dreamers, visionaries, poets, artists, world changers, leaders, and much more. I look forward with excitement to the many testimonies that this book is going to birth. God is doing a kingdom reset, and you have the privilege of having someone with a map. Your journey does not have to be the happenstance of previous generations.

Foreword
From The Heart of A Mother – Jennifer Roscher

My greatest desire has always been to be a mother. As a young women, I had plans for my life. I had goals mapped out the way I wanted them to go. I was trying to create my own destiny for God. My plans did not go as I imagine they would. As a result, my husband and I walked through years of pain from not conceiving. God used those years to build in me his heart for children, to teach me the value of children, and the gift that they are to us. God gave me greater revelation of what it means to steward and to train up our children in the way they should go, and to trust Him in the process. God was cultivating destiny all along in my life.

Cultivating Destiny from the Womb by Apostle Taquetta Baker, Shannon White, and Brandy Reese is powerful! Each of these authors bring their own uniqueness to this book through the wells God has cultivated in within them. This book is full of wisdom, power and revelation that is straight from God's word. This book is not just a casual read, but a training manual for us as parents, as well as for anyone desiring to see this generation and future generations walking in destiny with their God. We must grab hold of the truth found in God's word about our children and as our roles as parents!

Psalm 127:3-4 *Children are a gift from the Lord; They are a reward from him. Children born to a young man are like arrows in a Warriors hands.*

This book reveals that our children are not only gifts but weapons! We must steward them and train them. The enemy wants us to remain lax in the way we view our children. He does not want us to become equipped in our God-given authority and roles as their parents, because he knows the ground he will lose if they walk in their destiny life with God.

Cultivating Destiny From The Womb is an excellent resource for what destiny entails and teaching parents how to train children to walk in destiny. It explores

- Biblical teaching regarding how God's desire to use our children for his glory while they are young
- Our roles and purpose as parents and what the Bible says about training our children.
- The schemes of the enemy regarding our children, and what demonic spirits that come against them.

God spoke over and ordained our children to walk in destiny with him before they were formed in the womb. It is our responsibility as their parents to cultivate destiny in them, as well as search out with the Lord, who he says they are and train them accordingly. We cannot simply hope they will fall into their God identity. We need to be aware of the fact that we have an enemy who wants to steal, kill and destroy our children's destiny. We must be diligent. We must train them.

This book teaches us our authority as parents. It is a tool for us that equips us so we can take our post has governors in our homes, over our atmospheres, and over our kids. Lets cultivate destiny in our kids and our homes as a lifestyle! Lets keep that holy fire burning into the next generation! Decreeing your parental governing SHIFT even now!

Shift!

Shifted into Destiny Cultivation
Minister Shannon White's Testimony

"Mrs. White, they told me to pray…. *but it doesn't work.*" This was the truth from a twelve-year-old student in my office that shook me to my core. These eleven words equaling one sentence changed my entire life. I served as a youth minister, was raised in church, and was loving my first year as a professional school counselor, but it was at this very fragile moment that it felt like heaven came and dumped a divine gold nugget right in my lap. I struggled to respond, my voice quivered in attempts to give the politically correct answer due to separation of church and state. Yet all I could say was *"You're right."* This led to a brief conversation about how faith without works is dead and must go together, but more importantly it led to a revelation that something was missing for our young people. Day after day in my school I saw children wearing crosses, WWJD bracelets, and youth group t-shirts; yet they faced the exact same struggles of someone who had never stepped foot into a church. My question became, "What was missing?" Where was the disconnect?

Fast forward to the next year when I had a new baby and it was like God was sending smoke signals for me to get this message. A woman at my church who I respected dearly told me, *"Make sure you teach him about life too.* I was very good at teaching my kids about church, that I forgot to teach them how to do life." Finally, I got it. The disconnect is that many of us are good at doing church, but our kids do not know how to personally access the fruit or truth of God on their level. After that understanding I went on a hunt and made a vow to myself to teach my child God's word early so he could know God's truth on his level. My philosophy was if he can naturally learn and sing difficult songs from the radio verbatim, why can't he learn the words of the Bible at the same time? I began researching for toddler books that would have actual scriptures in them and I could not find any. It was at this time that I felt a nudge from the Holy Spirit to begin creating practical tools to help deposit the word of God into our children from birth. I considered that if scientists have proven that children can recognize songs sung to them or voices spoken to them in utero, what would happen if we declared scriptures over them in utero? In the Bible, John jumped in his mom's womb at the presence of Jesus. I wanted this depth of revelation for my child from the womb. As I sought God for insight on how to cultivate my child's destiny from the womb while also instilling the presence of God and covenant with him from the womb, I realized that my assignment as the mother of my son was to start teaching him about Jesus at a strong two years old, because if I did not do it, the enemy would surely be trying to teach my son about him and his ways. And I surely was not having that.

As I pursued God, helped me write a couple of books to help my son. During the time of publication, my son started preschool and started to have trouble. My son was warm, cuddly, funny, inquisitive, intelligent, and energetic, yet the teachers who bragged on these same adjectives also began to describe him in four letter words! They would say your son CAN'T do this, and he WON'T do this, and maybe he has ADHD. The cycle of these sentences continued until one day in my prayer corner I said, "God tell me what to do?" I see these teenagers who are active in church struggling in my school and my own son getting bad reports so what is missing? What should I do? I was frustrated, embarrassed, and starting to feel hopeless because I saw the moms coming into my office for the teens not understanding why their child was not showing up in a godly way at school. I became concerned that this was a prophecy for my son's future. The moms that came into my office did not understand their children's behavior because their child was involved in youth group, respectful, kind, and helpful, however, they were struggling with peers, choices, identity, and self-esteem. This started to also become my reality until I said enough is enough - God tell me what to do! His response was simple. He said, *"You need to train him."* From that day forward the Holy Spirit has taught me what it meant to intentionally train my child, and everything has shifted. It has been four years of training my children, as well as, some teen mentees from my community. God has consistently impressed upon my heart, how starting early is critical to the survival, and success of our spiritual inheritance. I have since given birth to a daughter. I train my children to experience God on their level so that they can find him to be more than a story, tradition, or myth. I need him to be God to them; therefore, I partner with heaven to create atmospheres and teachable moments that allow God to work and prove himself to my son and daughter. As a result, my son and I pray together in the Spirit, he dreams dreams, prophesies, and owns his own relationship with Christ. Are my children perfect? No, they are human, just like me and you. We are not called to be perfect. We are called to be holy and partner in covenant relationship with God where he can transform us and evolve his identity in and through us. As I work with my son, I have been divinely privileged to witness in my own his transformation, as well as the teens I have worked with. Using the understanding that our children's destiny cannot wait to be uncovered and trained, I recognize and PREACH that destiny must start in the womb. There is no time to waste. DESTINY IS NOW! IT IS EVERYDAY! IT is when we are considering having children, procreating, and carrying them in the womb, and nurturing and training them throughout life.

Using YouTube videos, songs, bath time, and his bad choices are all moments that God allows me to personally introduce who he is to my children. I even have the benefit of receiving from my child as he hears from God and speaks into my life. Being able to see the fruit of a *Deuteronomy 11:19-21* environment in my home has truly been a godly reinforcement in my life and family regarding the power of cultivating destiny from the womb.

Deuteronomy 11:18-21 (New International Version): Fix these words of mine in your hearts and minds; tie them as symbols on your hands and bind them on your foreheads. Teach them to your children, talking about them when you sit at home and when you walk along the road, when you lie down and when you get up. Write them on the doorframes of your houses and on your gates, so that your days and the days of your children may be many in the land the Lord swore to give your ancestors, as many as the days that the heavens are above the earth.

I will continue to live God's command with the expectation that my children's destinies are not something to attain for the future. It is something that heaven wants to partner with now so their lives can bear much fruit and bring them closer to our God. As I have SHIFTED into this being the lifestyle of me and

4

my child, I now help parents cultivate their child's destiny from the womb through my ministry Kingdom Convos. I declare that you and your seed will be SHIFTED through the revelation in this book as Dr. Taquetta, Brandie and I share insight on how to cultivate destiny from the womb. **SHIFT RIGHT NOW! SHIFT!**

God's Purpose for Parenting

Being an anti-Christ society and being culture driven, has SHIFTED us into waiting on children to form their personalities and display gifts and talents, before we start to explore who they are to be in the earth and speaking over their lives. Often what we are speaking is rooted in what they can do well and not in relations to what God has said about them.

We do not realize that by the time children begin to form a personality and display gifts and talents, generational curses, patterns, and propensities have already taken root in their DNA, identities, personalities, souls and bloodlines, and family familiar spirits have begun to commune and influence their character, nature, and desires.

With perversion and a self-idolatrous nature at an all-time high, YOUNG children are rejecting the very nature of their identity, thus dictating to parents, courts, and society who they should and want to be, what they should be called, and how they want to be identified as in the earth. Parents, courts, and society think they are helping the child by adhering to their wishes, but really are allowing generational transgressions, strongholds, and familiar spirits to steal, kill, and destroy the godly nature, identity, and destiny of children.

Parents are gatekeepers of the family!

Fathers – Men are responsible for gatekeeping the entire family through the vision God gives him for the family. Fathers are responsible for loving, protecting, and being financially breadwinner and pre-visionary for the family. Fathers are strategically aligned and chosen under God as governmental headship of the family for the purposes of providing godly covering regarding the visions and destinies that God gives the family and every individual of the family.

Mothers – Women are gatekeepers to birthing, nurturing, and co-laboring with the husband in covering the family. When a seed or a vision is planted in a woman, she – by divine design – can birth that thing forth. Women are key to birthing the child, then gatekeeping their lives such that they birth forth, and become the vision and destiny of God in the earth. Women then nurture the family and each child, and co labor with the father to develop, train, equip, and cultivate that family's and each child's vision and destiny so they can become who God has desires in the earth.

Worldly courts and governments were never intended to override God's kingdom government and design and family. Aside from paying taxes and respecting the laws of the land, God's people were never to rely on the world's systems for identity, destiny, instruction, guidance, provision. We were always meant to rule in the earth in dominion and gate keep life through God's laws, standards, and government.

When parents are not divinely gatekeeping the family, the household, bloodline, and the children are exposed to all kinds of toxins, weeds, tares, ideologies, evils, dangers, that can stifle or abort godly vision and destiny. God placed man and woman over families to govern in dominion when he created the earth.

Genesis 1:27-31 *So God created man in his own image, in the image of God created he him; male and female created he them. And God blessed them, and God said unto them, Be fruitful, and multiply, and replenish the earth, and subdue it: and have dominion over the fish of the sea, and over the fowl of the air, and over every living thing that moveth upon the earth.*

And God said, Behold, I have given you every herb bearing seed, which is upon the face of all the earth, and every tree, in the which is the fruit of a tree yielding seed; to you it shall be for meat. And to every beast of the earth, and to every fowl of the air, and to every thing that creepeth upon the earth, wherein there is life, I have given every green herb for meat: and it was so. And God saw every thing that he had made, and, behold, it was very good. And the evening and the morning were the sixth day.

Genesis 2:15-18 *And the Lord God took the man, and put him into the garden of Eden to dress it and to keep it. And the Lord God commanded the man, saying, Of every tree of the garden thou mayest freely eat: But of the tree of the knowledge of good and evil, thou shalt not eat of it: for in the day that thou eatest thereof thou shalt surely die. And the Lord God took the man, and put him into the garden of Eden to dress it and to keep it. And the Lord God commanded the man, saying, Of every tree of the garden thou mayest freely eat: But of the tree of the knowledge of good and evil, thou shalt not eat of it: for in the day that thou eatest thereof thou shalt surely die. And the Lord God said, It is not good that the man should be alone; I will make him an help meet for him.*

Verse 21-25 *And the Lord God caused a deep sleep to fall upon Adam, and he slept: and he took one of his ribs, and closed up the flesh instead thereof; And the rib, which the Lord God had taken from man, made he a woman, and brought her unto the man. And Adam said, This is now bone of my bones, and flesh of my flesh: she shall be called Woman, because she was taken out of Man. Therefore shall a man leave his father and his mother, and shall cleave unto his wife: and they shall be one flesh. And they were both naked, the man and his wife, and were not ashamed.*

It was God's will that man and woman would procreate with fruitfulness and be generationally blessed – multiply – as they reigned in the earth. Man and woman were given clear vision to subdue and dominate in the earth; they were supplied all that they needed through the provision and strategy of God to do just that. They were even provided with clear instructions and boundaries of what to do, what not to do, of how to remain safe, protected and under the blessing of the Lord as a they conquered in the earth. This lets us know that God is concerned about us prospering. He is concerned about us being exactly who he designed us to be in the earth. He desires us to have and achieve the greatness that he has bestowed upon us. He wants us to achieve this through covenant marriage, through the blessing of our womb, through cultivation of family, and generationally as we expand and advance in the earth.

The challenge with God's concept is that it is not respected or even considered in many of our covenant marriages and families of today.

- God is not the head of many families and if he is, he is not often sought out for vision and cultivation of destiny for the family as a whole or for the individuals within the family.

- God is sought often for emergency assistance, necessity, or through a religious perception of works within a church or ministry. This is done more so than God really letting him govern as the head of a household, and then everything about the family being governed through his kingship.

- Many households do not have fathers. Most are governed by mothers who are trying to fill both roles for the children in the home.

- Many mothers are praying women, but still tend to operate through the world's system rather than God's strategic design for governing the household.

- Many women do well at their role, but not matter how much they provide and seek God who blesses them with great insight and vision, a woman cannot take the ordained place of a man in a home and vice versa. It just is not possible because of our makeup and design. God meant for a man to be a man and a father and he meant for a woman to be a woman and a mother. No matter how much we swap roles or alter our identity, the nature of us and God's role for us is never changing.

- Most children are raised in mixture – a mixed government – where they have a little bit of God, little bit of the world, little bit of the devil, little bit of man's ideologies. They are given mixed inferences on how to serve God, live for God, live in God. Children may be taken to church and even taught to pray and read their bible' some are cultivated to a degree in relationship with God. Yet many go to school, engage in the community, and pursue destiny through worldly and demonic systems, rather than a system solely rooted in God. Within these systems, they are given boundaries on how and when to serve God, so depending on how much they engage in religious systems, much of their life can be cultivated outside the will and presence of God, his principles and his kingdom. This is because the more the world SHIFTS into a self-absorbed mentality, God is taken out of the equation. He is taken out of schools, out of communities, out of organizations, out of business, out of economics, politics, and replaced with good intent, manmade ideas, idolatry, and demonic infrastructures. God hates mixture. He threw Adam and Eve out the garden because he had no toleration for mixture *(Study Genesis 3)*.

Look at what he tells the church of Laodicea for engaging in mixture.

Revelations 3:15-16 I know thy works, that thou art neither cold nor hot: I would thou wert cold or hot. So then because thou art lukewarm, and neither cold nor hot, I will spue thee out of my mouth.

Some people simply do not know that the ultimate KEY to happiness as the world calls it – a fulfilled life is what I call it – entails true covenant with God. Without the creator speaking to us whom he created, we are just hoping to get it right, rather than having clear downloads through covenant relationships with him, so we make sure a fruitful, multiply, subduing, dominion life is our portion.

John 10:7-10 *Then said Jesus unto them again, Verily, verily, I say unto you, I am the door of the sheep. All that ever came before me are thieves and robbers: but the sheep did not hear them. I am the door: by me if any man enter in, he shall be saved, and shall go in and out, and find pasture. The thief cometh not, but for to steal, and to kill, and to destroy: I am come that they might have life, and that they might have it more abundantly.*

Factor this into how the world is SHIFTING where children are dictating to the parent what they want to be, how they want to be, how they should be parented, etc., and we have a serious mess on our hands. WE NEED A SHIFT RIGHT NOW AND SOON! A serious and necessary SHIFT needs to occur within families where they are being governed by true heads of family as God designed. But even if there is only one parent in the home, or foster parents, caregivers etc., are governing the home, we need to SHIFT back to God being the head so that we know his plan for our family. This is especially true for the children. Children are God's blessing to us. His fruitful heritage resides with them. We must SHIFT back into seeing them for the blessings that they are and speaking over our families, and seed before children are even consummated, formed, and born or the world will continue to be striped of the very essence of what it means to be human, the image of God, and living in his purpose in the earth. May a SHIFT overtake you as you are engulfed in the revelation in this book. May you be awakened like never before to value children, know your authority in impacting their lives, and govern your power and dominion properly through the voice, plan, will, and purpose of the Lord and Savior Jesus Christ. SHIFT! SHIFT RIGHT NOW! SHIFT!

What Is Destiny?

This chapter revelation is from Taquetta Baker's *Sustaining the Vision Workbook.*

Destiny is not necessarily a destination or a goal we are trying to reach as those points of success are just destiny moments. Destiny, however, is a lifestyle of living in the purpose and plan God ordained for us at birth. Destiny is not just a moment with God but a journey in and with God. SHIFT!

A destiny moment is temporary success. A destiny lifestyle is lifetime success with constant destiny moments.

Destiny is not always easy. It requires strategic efficient work to maintain and sustain in destiny. Even people who were handed a destiny moment must work that moment to maintain a lifestyle of destiny. This is the reason a person keeps working once they have attained or succeeded in a particular area, or to a particular level. They are striving to maintain and sustain in what they have achieved.

Ephesians 2:10 The Amplified Bible For we are God's [own] handiwork (His workmanship), recreated in Christ Jesus, [born anew] that we may do those good works which God predestined (planned beforehand) for us [taking paths which He prepared ahead of time], that we should walk in them [living the good life which He prearranged and made ready for us to live].

Psalms 139:16 The Amplified Bible Your eyes saw my unformed substance, and in Your book all the days [of my life] were written before ever they took shape, when as yet there was none of them.

From these scriptures we recognize that at creation, God had already committed to walking in destiny with us. He made it part of our DNA, our very substance, and instilled it into the plans for our lives.

This is the reason many people achieve destiny things (money, fame, material goods, temporary happiness, rewards, success) without God, as he put these talents and gifts in them at birth. Yet despite attainment, many of these people are still unhappy, longing, and constantly searching and filling themselves up with things in effort to acquire fulfillment. This is because true destiny fulfillment can only come through and with God.

Destiny is not necessarily about what we can do or attain as this is a biproduct of destiny. This is the result of destiny.

Destiny is about:
- Who we are uniquely in God (Identity)
- Why we are to do what he has called us to do (Purpose)
- The reason we are meant to do and be whatever he has chosen us to be in life (Plan)

Jeremiah 1:5 *Before I formed thee in the belly I knew thee; and before thou camest forth out of the womb I sanctified thee, and I ordained thee a prophet unto the nations.*

Isaiah 49:1 Listen, O isles, unto me; and hearken, ye people, from afar; The Lord hath called me from the womb; from the bowels of my mother hath he made mention of my name.

Basically, destiny is more about:
- What makes you you?
- What reasons did God make you you?

In this case:
- What makes your child who they are?
- What reasons did God birth them in the earth?

Cultivating Destiny from The Womb

The world would say that identity is about being our authentic self and that destiny is what we make it. I contend that destiny is cultivated through a relationship with God – our creator. We are made in the unique image of him so we cannot attain destiny part from him. Through God's image, we obtain our identity, as *identity* began in the garden with Adam and Eve.

Genesis 1:26 And God said, Let us make man in our image, after our likeness: and let them have dominion over the fish of the sea, and over the fowl of the air, and over the cattle, and over all the earth, and over every creeping thing that creepeth upon the earth.

The Message Bible God spoke: "Let us make human beings in our image, make them reflecting our nature So they can be responsible for the fish in the sea, the birds in the air, the cattle, And, yes, Earth itself, and every animal that moves on the face of Earth."

God's Image - God Likeness				
Affinity	Agreement	Alikeness	Carbon	Clone
Copy	Dead Ringer	Depiction	Double	Fashion
Illusion	Model	Likeness	Model	Photocopy
Photograph	Picture	Replica	Representation	Reproduction
Resemblance	Sameness	Study	Uniformity	Xerox

Dictionary.com defines *identity* as:

1. the state or fact of remaining the same one or ones, as under varying aspects or conditions
2. the condition of being oneself or itself, and not another
3. condition or character as to who a person or what a thing is
4. the state or fact of being the same one as described
5. exact likeness in nature or qualities
6. an instance or point of sameness or likeness

My question to the world is, *"How can someone identify who they are or be their authentic self if they do not acknowledge who created them, who their creator is, and seek knowledge of who they are through him?"*

Proverbs 19:21 *Many plans are in a man's mind, but it is the Lord's purpose for him that will stand.*

Psalm 119:105 *Your word is a lamp to my feet, and a light to my path.*

Psalms 139:13-17 *For thou hast possessed my reins: thou hast covered me in my mother's womb. I will praise thee; for I am fearfully and wonderfully made: marvellous are thy works; and that my soul knoweth right well. My substance was not hid from thee, when I was made in secret, and curiously wrought in the lowest parts of the earth. Thine eyes did see my substance, yet being unperfect; and in thy book all my members were written, which in continuance were fashioned, when as yet there was none of them. How precious also are thy thoughts unto me, O God! How great is the sum of them!*

Through our identity, forms our unique purpose in God, which thus determines our destiny. As we build a covenant relationship with God, he reveals revelation regarding our destiny. He then provides revelation and strategy of how to unfold destiny as a lifestyle.

Psalms 16:11 *You will show me the path of life; In Your presence is fullness of joy; At Your right hand are pleasures forevermore.*

As we are obedient to plans God gives us, we begin to cultivate destiny in and through him. To cultivate destiny with God means to:

- To devote oneself in friendship, service, and covenant with God.
- To grow in God's biblical standards, character, nature, where we further evolve into the distinct image of God.
- To create a atmosphere, culture, climate, and lifestyle that glorifies God.
- To commune in prayer and daily living with God, where we learn who we are in him.
- To be educated, developed, trained, and equip to walk in destiny.
- To work the plan of destiny as a lifestyle.

Cultivating destiny really should start in the womb. We can discern this concept all throughout the Bible as God provides direction regarding the lives of children from the womb.

Prophet Jeremiah – God revealed to him that he was sanctified and ordained before he was born from so that he could be prophet to the nations.

Jeremiah 1:5-10 Before I formed thee in the belly I knew thee; and before thou camest forth out of the womb I sanctified thee, and I ordained thee a prophet unto the nations. Then said I, Ah, Lord God! behold, I cannot speak: for I am a child. Then said I, Ah, Lord God! behold, I cannot speak: for I am a child. But the Lord said unto me, Say not, I am a child: for thou shalt go to all that I shall send thee, and whatsoever I command thee thou shalt speak. Be not afraid of their faces: for I am with thee to deliver thee, saith the Lord. Then the Lord put forth his hand, and touched my mouth. And the Lord said unto me, Behold, I have put my words in thy mouth. See, I have this day set thee over the nations and over the kingdoms, to root out, and to pull down, and to destroy, and to throw down, to build, and to plant.

The Amplified Bible *Before I formed you in the womb I knew [and] approved of you [as My chosen instrument], and before you were born I separated and set you apart, consecrating you; [and] I appointed you as a prophet to the nations.*

<u>Sanctified</u> is *qâḏaš* in Hebrew and means:
1. to be (causatively, make, pronounce or observe as) clean (ceremonially or morally)
2. appoint, bid, consecrate, dedicate, defile, hallow, (be, keep) holy(-er, place)
3. keep, prepare, proclaim, purify, sanctify(-ied one, self), wholly

4. to consecrate, sanctify, prepare, dedicate, be hallowed, be holy, be sanctified, be separate

Ordain is nâṭan in Hebrew and means:
1. to give, used with greatest latitude of application (put, make, etc.)
2. add, apply, appoint, ascribe, assign, avenge, bestow
3. cast, cause, charge, commit, consider

Before Jeremiah was born, he was already set apart and prepared to walk in his purpose as a prophet to the nations. Jeremiah's mother is not mentioned in the Bible, but he mentions his father in Jeremiah 1:1 who was a high priest of Israel. Even though Jeremiah was a priest, God had to reveal Jeremiah's life purpose to him, and encourage him in knowing he was equipped for it. Imagine if Jeremiah's parents who served the Lord had been cultivating him in the consecration and ordination of the Lord that was already established in him before birth? Jeremiah would not have questioned God when God revealed who he was and what he wanted him to do. Jeremiah did not feel the people would receive him because he was young, but God had encouraged him. Had he been cultivated in his destiny from the womb, he would have embraced it and been ready to walk in it without hesitation.

Prophet Isaiah - Isaiah's purpose was instilled in the region from the womb.

Isaiah 49:1-4 *Listen, O isles (O Region), unto me; and hearken, ye people, from afar; The Lord hath called me from the womb; from the bowels of my mother hath he made mention of my name. And he hath made my mouth like a sharp sword; in the shadow of his hand hath he hid me, and made me a polished shaft; in his quiver hath he hid me; And said unto me, Thou art my servant, O Israel, in whom I will be glorified. And said unto me, Thou art my servant, O Israel, in whom I will be glorified. Then I said, I have laboured in vain, I have spent my strength for nought, and in vain: yet surely my judgment is with the Lord, and my work with my God.*

The prophet Isaiah declared to the people and spheres of his region that he was called from the womb, and commanded them to respond to what God put in them regarding him at birth. Through the revelation from God, Isaiah knew his prophetic mouth was a weapon - a sharp sword and that he was a polished arrow in the hands of God. He knew that he could be exactly who God desired because God was with him and was protecting him. This enabled him to prophetically govern during the most turbulent times of Judah's history. He had to release warnings, judgments, deliverance and salvation of God. But God had to reveal this to him. Even in his fear of being wretchedness and unworthy, he was willing to be used. Oh, how great it would be for him to have known this from the womb and for him to be able to declare it as he was being cultivated in his destiny and calling.

Sampson - Sampson knew his purpose and destiny from birth and was cultivated in it.

Judges 13:5 *For behold, you shall conceive and give birth to a son, and no razor shall come upon his head, for the boy shall be a Nazirite to God from the womb; and he shall begin to deliver Israel from the hands of the Philistines."*

Judges 13:7 *But he said to me, 'Behold, you shall conceive and give birth to a son, and now you shall not drink wine or strong drink nor eat any unclean thing, for the boy shall be a Nazirite to God from the womb to the day of his death.'"*

Judges 16:17 *So he told her all that was in his heart and said to her, "A razor has never come on my head, for I have been a Nazirite to God from my mother's womb. If I am shaved, then my strength will leave me and I will become weak and be like any other man."*

Sampson was clear in his purpose but was insecure in his identity. He dreaded being called from the womb. He felt the call was too difficult and demanded too much of him. Because of this perception, Sampson did not properly govern his life, his flesh, or his sphere of influence. He took risks with his destiny which caused the cutting of his locks, stifling of his strength, and the premature death of his destiny (***Study Judges 14-16***). This is where we must understand that cultivating destiny, a healthy identity, and dominion in our children are equally important. They must know what they are called to do and how to govern over what God has granted to their hands. As a lack of governing can stifle and abort their destiny. They must know how to joy and find joy in who God called them to be and to govern the value of their unique calling. If they do not have joy, they will constantly question God, question their purpose, and be reckless with the calling that is on their lives. In reading the story of Sampson, you will find that he fulfilled his call by perishing with the very people he was called to protect his people from. We want our children to live in the blessings, favor, harvest, and inheritance of destiny. We want them to experience the fruit of their labor rather than die with it. Helping your child find fulfillment in destiny is key to them thriving rather than surviving. It is key to them living abundantly in who God called them to be in the earth.

King David – This shephard was a heart chaser of God from his mother's womb.

1Samuel 13:14 *But now thy kingdom shall not continue: the Lord hath sought him a man after his own heart, and the Lord hath commanded him to be captain over his people, because thou hast not kept that which the Lord commanded thee.*

1Samuel 17:33-35 *But Saul replied, "You cannot go out against this Philistine to fight him. You are just a boy, and he has been a warrior from his youth." David replied, "Your servant has been tending his father's sheep, and whenever a lion or a bear came and carried off a lamb from the flock, I went after it, struck it down, and delivered the lamb from its mouth. If it reared up against me, I would grab it by its fur, strike it down, and kill it.*

Psalms 22:10 *Upon You I was cast from birth; You have been my God from my mother's womb.*

Psalms 139:13 *For You formed my inward parts; You wove me in my mother's womb.*

He was a young man after God's own heart. In his youth, he was found tending sheep, while being groomed as a warrior and king with the Lord. He was clear in his identity, and when anointed for destiny, he did not waver. He welcomed it and further positioned himself for it. David often made mention that he knew he was God's and that he was called from the womb. He at times used this revelation to obtain favor and mercy from the Lord.

***

John the Baptist – This leaping baby was called to pave the way for Jesus.

Luke 1:15 *For he will be great in the sight of the Lord; and he will drink no wine or liquor, and he will be filled with the Holy Spirit while yet in his mother's womb.*

Luke 1:35-39 *And the angel answered and said unto her, The Holy Ghost shall come upon thee, and the power of the Highest shall overshadow thee: therefore also that holy thing which shall be born of thee shall be called the Son of God. And, behold, thy cousin Elisabeth, she hath also conceived a son in her old age: and this is the sixth month with her, who was called barren. For with God nothing shall be impossible. And Mary said, Behold the* *handmaid of the Lord; be it unto me according to thy word. And the angel departed from her.*

Luke 1:41 And it came to pass, that, when Elisabeth heard the salutation of Mary, the babe leaped in her womb; and Elisabeth was filled with the Holy Ghost:

John 1:26-28 I baptize with water," John replied, "but among you stands One you do not know. He is the One who comes after me, the straps of whose sandals I am not worthy to untie." All this happened at Bethany beyond the Jordan, where John was baptizing.

John the Baptist was chosen by God to pave the way for Jesus's coming. He confirmed his coming and calling in the womb to Mary by leaping in his mom's belly. He was a miracle baby for Elisabeth was barren but then blessed with a child in her old age. He was filled with the Holy Ghost in his mother's womb. This is a key for parents as often we wait until children are of age before they are filled with the Holy Spirit. But children can be filled in the womb. They can know God's presence and be cultivated in God's presence in the womb. I would encourage mothers to seek God for the infilling of the Holy Spirit when they are pregnant and spend time praying, praise, worshiping, and study God's word during pregnancy and even instilling a love for these God covenant practices in their child from the womb.

Jesus Christ – Our savior was called before conception to redeem the world of all sins.

Luke 1:30-35 *And the angel said unto her, Fear not, Mary: for thou hast found favour with God. And, behold, thou shalt conceive in thy womb, and bring forth a son, and shalt call his name Jesus. He shall be great, and shall be called the Son of the Highest: and the Lord God shall give unto him the throne of his father David: And he shall reign over the house of Jacob for ever; and of his kingdom there shall be no end. Then said Mary unto the angel, How shall this be, seeing I know not a man? And the angel answered and said unto her, The Holy Ghost shall come upon thee, and the power of the Highest shall overshadow thee: therefore also that holy thing which shall be born of thee shall be called the Son of God.*

Luke 2:21 *And when eight days had passed, before His circumcision, His name was then called Jesus, the name given by the angel before He was conceived in the womb.*

Mary knew about Jesus' calling before she was pregnant. An angel provided her with the destiny plan for Jesus. You do not have to wonder if you have a king in your belly. God will give you the plan for your child. He will send messenger angels to share the information or give it to you directly. God will tell you about your king, give you his purpose in life, and give you strategy for how to cultivate your child in destiny.

Apostle Paul – Who would have believed that the Apostle Paul, once a persecutor of Christians, was called from his mother's womb to preach the gospel.

Galatians 1:11-15 But I certify you, brethren, that the gospel which was preached of me is not after man. For I neither received it of man, neither was I taught it, but by the revelation of Jesus Christ. For ye have heard of my conversation in time past in the Jews' religion, how that beyond measure I persecuted the church of God, and wasted it: And profited in the Jews' religion above many my equals in mine own nation, being more exceedingly zealous of the traditions of my fathers. But when it pleased God, who separated me from my mother's womb, and called me by his grace, To reveal his Son in me, that I might preach him among the heathen; immediately I conferred not with flesh and blood: Neither went I up to Jerusalem to them which were apostles before me; but I went into Arabia, and returned again unto Damascus.

Romans 1:1 Paul, a servant of Jesus Christ, called to be an apostle, separated unto the gospel of God.

If Paul had known the revelation of his destiny as a child, he probably would have lived a very different life. It was not until his divine encounter with God on the road to Damascus in Acts 9, that his life SHIFTED to following and preaching Jesus. It was sometime after this that God reveal to him that he had been called from the womb. Thankfully Apostle Paul complied immediately with God and began to instantly walk in his calling. This is key for those of you that will read this book and be challenged because you were not cultivated in destiny from the womb. It is never too late to journey in a destiny lifestyle with God. So even as you are seeking revelation for your unborn children and children and youth you already have, ask God what your calling is and align with it IMMEDIATELY – SHIFT IMMEDIATELY INTO DESTINY.

You can be an example to your children of:

- ✓ How to covenant with God
- ✓ Commune with God
- ✓ Hear God for life vision and strategy
- ✓ How to be trained and equipped in destiny with God
- ✓ How to be cultivated in a destiny lifestyle with God
- ✓ How to journey in sustaining successful destiny with God.

Decreeing it is so for you right now!

Shift!

Benefits of Cultivating Destiny from The Womb

When we cultivate our children in destiny, we train, and prepare them in what God is saying for their lives, activate them in that by aligning their character, nature, talents, abilities, and lives in what God is speaking. They are being given clear revelation, direction, and guidance regarding their purpose in the earth, how to walk in it and how to govern it. Destiny being cultivated from the womb provides:

- ❖ Foundation, direction, and guidance for a child to walk through.

- ❖ Fortification where the enemy and wicked people cannot talk your child out of or steal their identity.

- ❖ With life fruit and spiritual production that is abundantly sustainable, and more sufficient as your child is clear about who they are, whose they are and how to govern it.

- ❖ Godly boundaries and standards that limits your child's risk for walking in idolatry and worldliness.

- ❖ Keeps the blessings, name and kingdom of God in the family line. *Genesis 22:18* *And in thy seed shall all the nations of the earth be blessed; because thou hast obeyed my voice.*

- ❖ Grand opportunity for God to be glorified from generation to generation, which is God's ultimate purpose for family and children.

Psalms 102:18 This will be written for the generation to come, That a people yet to be created may praise the LORD.

Psalms 145:4 One generation shall praise thy works to another, and shall declare thy mighty acts.

Psalms 100:5 For the LORD [is] good; his mercy [is] everlasting; and his truth [endureth] to all generations.

Luke 1:50 And his mercy [is] on them that fear him from generation to generation.

Psalms 78:4 We will not hide [them] from their children, shewing to the generation to come the praises of the LORD, and his strength, and his wonderful works that he hath done.

Daniel 4:3 How great [are] his signs! and how mighty [are] his wonders! his kingdom [is] an everlasting kingdom, and his dominion [is] from generation to generation.

Psalms 71:18 Now also when I am old and gray headed, O God, forsake me not; until I have shewed thy strength unto [this] generation, [and] thy power to every one [that] is to come.

God desires relationship with children just as he does with adults.

Mark 10:13-16 And they brought young children to him, that he should touch them: and his disciples rebuked those that brought them. But when Jesus saw it, he was much displeased, and said unto them, Suffer the little children to come unto me, and forbid *them not: for of such is the kingdom of God. Verily I say unto you, Whosoever shall not receive the kingdom of God as a little child, he shall not enter therein. And he took them up in his arms, put his hands upon them, and blessed them.*

Verse 13-14 The Message Bible *The people brought children to Jesus, hoping he might touch them. The disciples shooed them off. But Jesus was irate and let them know it: "Don't push these children away. Don't ever get between them and me. These children are at the very center of life in the kingdom.*

We see Jesus expressing indignation to the disciples for rebuking those who brought the children to him. He told them not to get between him and the children. Jesus also expressed that children are the heart of the kingdom. They are the fruit of the kingdom of God. To separate them from the kingdom is an abomination to the point that those who do will not be enter into it.

We need to stop and consider how our eternity is in jeopardy when we do not teach our kids how to have a relationship with God, and make sure they encounter and live for him. When we consider this revelation, we would take our roles as parents more seriously, where we would cry out for Jesus to touch them, bless them, enable them to live for him. I decree a convicting SHIFT is coming upon every reader that they would suffer not the children to come to the Lord. SHIFT! SHIFT RIGHT NOW!

Costs of Not Cultivating Destiny from the Womb

Some of this chapter revelation is from Taquetta Baker's *Sustaining the Vision Workbook.*

When destiny is not cultivated from the womb, we tend to raise our children through talents rather than their spiritual gifts. It is the latter that grooms them in their purpose and calling.

Talents
Talents are skills and abilities that you do well. All talents are not listed in the bible, but are a grace, uniqueness, and ability to do something with supernatural uniqueness and ability that others may or may not have, Even if another has a similar talent, it is not a replication of you or your talent. An example of a talent is playing a musical instrument, singing, being a great athlete, intellectual capabilities, etc. If you do it well and it comes naturally to you, it is probably a talent from God.

Gifts
Spiritual gifts are repeatedly mentioned in the Bible. They are gifts empowered by God's Holy Spirit. There are gifts that God has given for the purposes of saving the lost, bringing deliverance and healing to people, lands, and regions, and establishing God's kingdom in the earth.

Romans 12:6-8 Having then gifts differing according to the grace that is given to us, whether prophecy, let us prophesy according to the proportion of faith; Or ministry, let us wait on our ministering: or he that teacheth, on teaching; Or he that exhorteth, on exhortation: he that giveth, let him do it with simplicity; he that ruleth, with diligence; he that sheweth mercy, with cheerfulness.

1Corinthians 12:28-31 And God hath set some in the church, first apostles, secondarily prophets, thirdly teachers, after that miracles, then gifts of healings, helps, governments, diversities of tongues. Are all apostles? are all prophets? are all teachers? are all workers of miracles? Have all the gifts of healing? do all speak with tongues? do all interpret? But covet earnestly the best gifts: and yet shew I unto you a more excellent way.

1Corinthians 12: 8-10 For to one is given by the Spirit the word of wisdom; to another the word of knowledge by the same Spirit; To another faith by the same Spirit; to another the gifts of healing by the same Spirit; To another the working of miracles; to another prophecy; to another discerning of spirits; to another divers kinds of tongues; to another the interpretation of tongues:

Spiritual Gifts in the Bible:

Romans 2:6-8 prophecy, serving, teaching, exhortation, giving leadership, and mercy

1Corinthians 12:8-10 word of wisdom, word of knowledge, faith, gifts of healing, miracles, prophecy, discernment of spirits, tongues, interpretation of tongues

34

1Corinthians 12:28 *apostle, prophet, teacher, miracles, various kinds of healings, helps, administration, tongues*

We can ask the Holy Spirit to give us and our children spiritual gifts, and the Holy Spirit can teach us and our children how to operate in them. As growth takes place in these gifts, our skill level increases over time.

Almost always the first gift we will see in children is the discernment of spirits. Pay close attention to how your children, even as a baby and toddler, respond to various individuals. Do not dismiss it as "just a kid" response to a person, whether positive or negative.

Governmental Offices

Ephesians 4:11-13 And he gave some, apostles; and some, prophets; and some, evangelists; and some, pastors and teachers; For the perfecting of the saints, for the work of the ministry, for the edifying of the body of Christ: Till we all come in the unity of the faith, and of the knowledge of the Son of God, unto a perfect man, unto the measure of the stature of the fulness of Christ.

These are governmental offices that God gave as gifts for the equipping of the body of Christ. God installs these offices in us at birth. If he does not install this office in us or our children, we cannot promote ourselves to this office or go to a Christian school, learn these gifts, expected to be positioned into these offices. Either they are in us – part of our ordained identity - or they are not. In the contemporary church, we often see individuals doing exactly what was just mentioned and pursuing training in one of the five offices. A person can become educated in the ways of an office, but there is no comparison to those who God has equipped for the office.

These five offices are for the purposes of providing spiritual authorities that can empower, equip, and release the body of Christ in their giftings and callings, while asserting and maintaining Godly jurisdiction against principalities and strongholds that would strive to negatively influence people, lands, and regions. A person can be apostolic, prophetic, evangelistic, pastoral, or a teacher but not have a divine ordination for the governmental office.

The office provides the ability to govern and legislate against demonic entities, spiritual realms, regions, and within the constructs of assemblies, businesses, and communities. As a parent, you will need to learn how these offices operate in order to teach your children how to operate in them. Also If God has not called you or your child to this, you all can encounter a lot of hardship and tribulation by operating in these positions as those who have the offices, have a grace to contend and endure the warfare that comes with these offices. If your child is called, even at a young age, that child will be covered by grace.

2Corinthians 4:8-17 We are troubled on every side, yet not distressed; we are perplexed, but not in despair; Persecuted, but not forsaken; cast down, but not destroyed; Always bearing about in the body the dying of the Lord Jesus, that the life also of Jesus might be made manifest in our body. For we which live are always delivered unto death for Jesus' sake, that the life also of Jesus might be made manifest in our mortal flesh. So then death worketh in us, but life in you. We having the same spirit of faith, according as it is written, I believed, and therefore have I spoken; we also believe, and therefore speak; Knowing that he which raised up the Lord Jesus shall raise up us also by Jesus, and shall present us with you. For all things are for your sakes, that the abundant grace might through the thanksgiving of many redound to the glory of God. For which cause we faint not; but though our outward man perish, yet the inward man is renewed day by day. For our light affliction, which is but for a moment, worketh for us a far more exceeding and eternal weight of glory; While we look not at the things which are seen, but at the things which are not seen: for the things which are seen are temporal; but the things which are not seen are eternal.

As believers, we endure some of this for the gospel sake, those in governmental offices live their callings daily as a lifestyle and mandate. It can be a constant spiritual and natural battle depending on a season of destiny. Imagine striving to endure this type of lifestyle warfare daily without God creating you for this position? It would be a horrific life of unnecessary hardship.

If God called you or your child to these offices and you or your child do not embrace them, it opens the door to a spiritual struggle that will manifest in the natural. The principalities and powers in these jurisdictions are contending and warring for these realms and you and your child will feel and experience the weight of that whether the calling is embraced or not. This is the reason some children have a very tumultuous childhood. They are called to these offices but are not cultivated in them. The devil knows they are called so he attacks them at a young age to get them so bound where they do not want to live, let alone live for God. When we and our children accept our calling, the grace to contend is upon us, and hell is terrorized by us and our children instead of the other way around.

Sevenfold Spirit Of The Lord

In addition to being born with talents and gifts, born in gifted offices, and pursuing supernatural gifts, the Spirit of the Lord can rest upon you and your children with an anointing and qualification to judge through the intellect and mind of God.

Isaiah 11:2 And the spirit of the Lord shall rest upon him, the spirit of wisdom and understanding, the spirit of counsel and might, the spirit of knowledge and of the fear of the Lord. And shall make him of quick understanding in the fear of the Lord: and he shall not judge after the sight of his eyes, neither reprove after the hearing of his ears: But with righteousness shall he judge the poor, and reprove with equity for the meek of the earth: and he shall smite the earth: with the rod of his mouth, and with the breath of his lips shall he slay the wicked.

Gifts Make Room

Proverbs 18:12 *says, "A man's gift maketh room for him, and bringeth him before great men."*

We tend to equate this scripture to our capabilities and talents. However, the word gift in this scripture means, "offerings, presents, reward, gift." It is really when we are giving our gifts as a blessing to others that makes room for us and SHIFTS us into greatness. This is essential to recognizing that our gifts and talents have purpose. They are to empower someone's life, the earth, and the world at large. We must pursue God for how he desires us and our children to impact others, the earth, and the world, so that our remnant can reap the rewards of our destiny.

Often, what is making room for children is their talents. They are receiving rewards and trophies for playing sports, for participating in school programs, or for getting good grades in school. Rarely is the spotlight shown for talents and how it impacts God's kingdom and peoples' lives. They are seen more as entertainment and opportunities for parents to boast of their achievements than kingdom vessels who have purpose in the earth. We even make put pressure on children to succeed for the purposes of SHIFTING us out of our poverty state or so they can purchase us things we cannot afford to pay for on our own. For many children, this becomes the focus of their reason for succeeding. It becomes their destiny plan, while their true purpose gets tossed to the waist side. Please understand that this is more slave labor than a child's purpose. We must make sure that we are not making our children serve us as it relates to their purpose rather than serving God. We must also seek God for who and how they are to impact through their destiny, where they do not get stuck operating in talents but never achieving their calling.

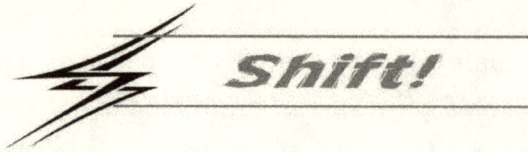

Shift!

Gifts Versus Destiny

One of the revelations I have received is that destiny is not a gift or talent, it is a function of your purpose and calling. We can narrow down what our destiny may be by what we and our children do well, but that does not necessarily mean that is the function of destiny. Some people stumble upon or into destiny and some strive to pursue a desired dream, or a portion of destiny based on personal aptitudes and strengths that may or may not unveil or SHIFT them into destiny.

Dr. Taquetta Baker's Destiny Testimony

Growing up, I was supported in my talents, but not groomed in the function of destiny. As a young child, I was very smart. I loved to dance so for several years, my aunt had me attending different genres of dance classes. After learning how to play basketball, I stopped attending dance classes and started attending basketball camps, clubs and the like. I played basketball throughout junior high, high school, and into college. I was not groomed for college though I was encouraged to go to college. I surely was not groomed for a career or destiny.

I was groomed to go to church, survive, be strong, persevere, never give up, be a woman that did not need anyone for anything, stand on my own two feet, have great work ethic, be the best that I can be and to take care of myself. These attributes were engrained in me, and have helped sustain me in destiny, but did not help me to know my destiny.

In college, I chose the major psychology because I was always intrigued by why people do what they do. After undergrad, I pursued a counseling degree as I was wise, a good listener, and could help people solve life problems. This became my career path and what I thought was my destiny, so I began to walk in it. I have had numerous counseling and case management jobs, but I have spent much of my professional career in the job function of a behavior consultant.

Professionally, I do perform some counseling, but mostly I provide consultation and skills building to mentally and physically challenged people of all ages. This would have been my destiny path, had I not entered a relationship with Jesus, and realized that counseling is a judgment gift that rest upon me, consultation is a talent, but this is not my destiny.

As I really became saved and began to journey with Jesus as a lifestyle, everything I thought about my life began to SHIFT. Aside from obtaining a master's degree, much of what I thought was my destiny path and what I would accomplish in life, has never unfolded. What God has revealed and caused me to do in life was never my expectation or anything I would have chosen or fathomed for myself. I would have never chosen any of this because I was not groomed in relationship with God, I was groomed to go to church. I was not groomed to seek God in destiny nor that was my destiny rooted in God.

As I journeyed in relationship with God, I still stumbled into my destiny. Though I consistently attended church and utilized my gifts, talents, and strengths in church, I was not groomed in destiny. I was the main person talking about the importance of destiny at the church I attended. But works, talent and position, were the forefront of the church, so it was very difficult to get anyone to really listen and cultivate a lifestyle of destiny into us as sheep.

My obedience to whatever God told me to do and what he revealed and unveiled as I journeyed with him, SHIFTED me into destiny. I did not even know this was what was unfolding until I was committed to God. I possessed a yearning that all I wanted to do was please God and be in his will. Then I began to realize that what he was having me to do as we walked through life in covenant together was my destiny lifestyle and I was walking out my life's purpose in him.

By that time, I was preaching, teaching, delivering, healing, and saving others, while helping them to explore and SHIFT into their destiny and life's purpose. The more I walked in this, the more my purpose was revealed and became defined. I also learned how to pursue gifts of the Holy Spirit and use them to empower the talents and skills that were within me. Because I did not know until I was doing destiny, that my destiny and calling was being identified, I had many seasons where I just called myself a humble servant, then I slowly took on the title of minister, then I thought, and others called me a prophet, then I learned and realized through the counsel and direction of God that I was an Apostle and that my calling was to raise up kingdom shifters for his glory. Had I been groomed to journey with God in relationship, I could have bypassed a lot of trials, seasons of the unknowns and error and been groomed in destiny from a young age.

Even as an Apostle, I use my counseling gift that rested upon me to judge, but it is not the sum of me. It is only a fraction of my destiny - not the consumption. This could very well be the reason many famous people are so unfulfilled. They have pursued their dreams and get to operate and succeed in their gifts and talents, but that is not their full purpose in life - it is not the consumption of them. After they have attained a measure of success, many of them are still empty as they strive to find real purpose. Without a relationship with God, many engage in a lot of good works and services of helping others through their financial wealth, giving encouraging talks and taking on causes through their famous platforms, but rarely is this purpose or fulfilling.

We wonder how someone with lots of money, can buy and have whatever they want, can still be lonely, unfulfilled, constantly error or have trials, lack focus and platforms sustainment, etc. it is because what they are doing and have done all their lives is not destiny. It is works of gifting but not works of destiny. Because God created us, and we are made in his image, we cannot successfully journey in our destiny and calling without a relationship with him. Without a relationship with God, our talents and gifts can produce success and prosperity, but it will not produce destiny fulfillment. Destiny fulfillment can only come from journeying with God in a destiny lifestyle.

Proverbs 19:21 *There are many devices in a man's heart; nevertheless the counsel of the LORD, that shall stand.*

Devices in the Hebrew is *mahăšâ̱ḇâ* or *machashebeth* and means:

44

1. contrivance (plots, schemes, plans), i.e. (concretely) a texture
2. machine (workings), or (abstractly) intention,
3. plan (whether bad, a plot; or good, advice): — cunning (work), curious work
4. device(-sed), imagination, invented, means, purpose, thought/s

   - Good thoughts, ideas, and plans do not equate to destiny.
   - Good imaginations and dreams do not equate to destiny.
   - Good plans, cunning and curious works, plots and schemes do not equate to destiny.
   - Good works and working hard while producing great success do not equate to destiny.
   - Just because you thought it and it produced does not equate to destiny.

New American Standard Bible *There are many plans in a man's heart; nevertheless, the counsel of the LORD that shall stand.*

If it is not the thoughts and mind of God for you, it is not destiny.

Jeremiah 29:11 *For I know the thoughts that I think toward you, saith the LORD, thoughts of peace, and not of evil, to give you an expected end.*

The word *thoughts* in this scripture is the same word as devices in **Proverbs 19:21**. God's thoughts must govern our lives. We cannot do this without relationship with him – Our Creator.

You or your child's function may be minister, business owner, counselor, pastor, CEO, prophet, psalmist, and more and there are great giftings and talents intertwined in these areas, but make sure you and your child are in purpose and not talent and gifted works. You all can work a gift or talent and not be in destiny or in purpose. Purpose gives the gift and talent meaning and fulfillment. Purpose is what enables us to walk in, unveil, and evolve in destiny. You and your child do not want to leave this world being known as a good people who did a lot of great things, and touched a lot of people, but never fulfilled destiny.

Proverbs 19:21 The Message Bible We humans keep brainstorming options and plans, but God's purpose prevails.

Shift!

The Difference Between Parenting and Training

One of the most memorized parenting scriptures is **Proverbs 22:6 New International Bible** *Train up a child in the way he should go: and when he is old, he will not depart from it.*

While this speaks to a command of the Lord, the interpretation of this command typically leaves much to be desired. It appears to state that if you raise a child in the way they should go that when they get older, they will not leave the Christian faith. However, in society we consistently see children that have been raised in church or Christian households leaving the faith or having a weak relationship in God.

An examination of the verb God chose to use in this verse clarifies his vision for leading children in the way they "should go." There are two ways we can consider God's command for parents to train.

English definitions:
- Train – teach a particular skill or type of behavior through practice or instruction over a period of time.
- Parent – bring up and care for.

At a very basic level, the definitions of these words, suggests that many Christians parents are professionals at parenting but timid trainers.

Many Christian parents are professionals at parenting but timid trainers.

While both functions are undoubtedly important, it is enough to note that there is a difference between parenting and training. God in his wisdom asked parents to train, not necessarily parent, children in the way they should go so they would not depart.

Parents are amazing at parenting, loving, caring, cooking, chauffeuring, helping, clothing, and sheltering children. Yet, when it comes to training children's spirituality, many parents are intimidated or leave it to a youth group or pastor. This is a popular church understanding, but not a kingdom principle for passing the torch of faith in one's family.

While youth groups, pastors, and ministry teachers are invaluable to the growth of the body, the reality is that children only see these spiritual leaders for their personal growth perhaps once or twice a week. However, children see their parents every day. Parenting is important, but training is God's mentioned plan for our children's survival and success in the spirit realm.

Let's also briefly explore the second way to consider God's command for parents: the Greek lexicon definition of the word *train*.

Greek definition:
- Train - *chanaq* to narrow

Narrowing speaks to decreasing the scope of something. The narrowing of a child can pertain to the focus, gifts, schedule, or mindset of kingdom living being the standard of abundant life.

Nevertheless, whether the English or Greek definition is considered, God's expectations for equipping children in the way that should go require honing or focusing a behavior or action over a period of time. Therefore, by definition, we can conclude that God asks parents to stop just parenting and start training their child for kingdom living to sustain in their life.

Sidebar from Dr. K. Williams

When I was a little girl, I played teacher with my toys. I didn't just play teacher, I played special education teacher which is a role that did not exist in education at that time. With no insult intended to anyone and not terms I would ever use now, there were three kinds of people in my childhood. A person was normal, crippled, or retarded. When I played teacher, one of my dolls was retarded and one was crippled. I would ask my retarded doll a question and then tell the rest of my toys, "Now, be patient. She can answer." When I took the toys for recess, I reminded them to wait on my crippled doll so that she could catch up. Why am I sharing this? Pay attention to the games your children play as it will reveal clues about their destiny. In fact, their games are a good starting point for connecting them to opportunities that will help them develop. Remember that you are their first coach and their strongest advocate. Pay attention not only to what they do but to what they say. Ask inquisitive questions to let them explain what they are thinking or experiencing. Your child may talk about dreams before they can read or write, so it is up to you to journal those dreams. Look for the characteristics behind their activities. Every good trainer has a procedure that has been proven over time. God not only trusted your child with gifts, he trusted you to be their Mommy or Daddy. You are chosen!

The Calling of God to Train Children in Destiny

Many people say there is no instruction manual for raising children; however, the Bible consistently gives God's vision for equipping the next generation to walk in the promises of God. As parents follow God's outline, they make room for their child to personally experience God and walk in their destiny.

Destiny does not start in adulthood. It begins in the womb, and it starts with parents sharing what they know or have experienced in Christ. In the same way that society calls parents to use their experiences to educate their child about ABC's or reading, God also calls parents to use their experiences to prepare their child for Kingdom Living.

Children being aware of their identity and destiny is so important to God that before the Israelites could enter their promise land, he gave parents a clarion call to sustain their heritage through their children. Since parents were the ones to first experience God's power and love, parents were reminded that God was holding them responsible for passing the truth of God down to their children. God spoke very clearly to the parents and as it was then, so it is now.

God does not change and neither has his intentions changed to use parents to facilitate an environment that shares the truth and power of God with children.

Deuteronomy 11:2-7 New International Version Remember today that your children were not the ones who saw and experienced the discipline of the LORD your God: his majesty, his mighty hand, his outstretched arm; the signs he performed and the things he did in the heart of Egypt, both to Pharaoh king of Egypt and to his whole country; what he did to the Egyptian army, to its horses and chariots, how he overwhelmed them with the waters of the Red Sea as they were pursuing you, and how the LORD brought lasting ruin on them. It was not your children who saw what he did for you in the wilderness until you arrived at this place, and what he did to Dathan and Abiram, sons of Eliab the Reubenite, when the earth opened its mouth right in the middle of all Israel and swallowed them up with their households, their tents and every living thing that belonged to them. But it was your own eyes that saw all these great things the LORD has done.

Children have not yet experienced the great things of God. For this reason, God makes it clear that the prerequisite for parents training children for destiny is for parents to remember how great and awesome their God has been to them. It is only then that parents can fulfill God's vision for training and equipping their child in destiny. God in his sovereignty knew that questions would arise about how to equip children, so he went even further to give parents six practical ways to train and equip children in their destiny.

Deuteronomy 11:18-21 New International Bible

1. *Fix these words of mine in your hearts and minds; tie them as symbols on your hands and bind them on your foreheads*
2. *Teach them to your children*
3. *Talking about them when you sit at home and when you walk along the road*

4. *When you lie down*
5. *When you get up*
6. *Write them on the doorframes of your houses and on your gates so that your days and the days of your children may be many in the land the LORD swore to give your ancestors, as many as the days that the heavens are above the earth*

This vision that God has for a righteous home is echoed throughout the Bible and comes with a promise of many days. Who does not want that for their child? It is a no-brainer. God consistently reminds parents about the power they have in order to equip their child in destiny and even ensures that parents know he is depending on them to raise up the next generation under them.

God intentionally placed scriptures and stories about parenting in the Bible for his people because he knew there would be some misunderstandings about his vision of equipping children. Many parents believe that bringing their child to Sunday school, youth group, conferences, or doing nightly family prayers are enough to equip their child in destiny but God is calling us to a deeper work. These things are not bad and are part of the bigger picture. Even as we all play a role in the body of Christ, God is calling parents deeper.

Proverbs 22:6 New International Bible *Train up a child in the way he should go: and when he is old, he will not depart from it.*

Many parents are pros at parenting, but timid when it comes to training. The word train in this verse comes from the Greek work *chanaq* meaning to narrow. The above scripture speaks to God's call for parents to go further than taking care of their child. It is a call for parents to narrow the focus of their child to know who they are and who God is amongst the clamor of life, society, and vices of the enemy that will confront them regularly.

Although we have set up effective organizations or ministries in the church, sometimes parents feel inadequate to train their child because they do not function as a pastor, youth minister, or apostle. The truth is that God has given his people everything they will need to fulfill each assignment he has placed to their hands. Parenting is indeed a ministry and, if parents seek God, his divine power will equip each parent with everything needed to fulfill their role as a minister to their child. This promise is for everyone who has received a faith through Jesus, including every believing parent.

2Peter 1:3 *His divine power has given us everything we need for a godly life through our knowledge of him who called us by his own glory and goodness.*

When a parent believes in Christ, not only does God give the parent everything they need to fulfill his purposes through them, but he also gives authority to do so. Through Christ Jesus every believer has been qualified to walk in authority in the earth. Many parents walk fearfully as they consider what could happen to their child due to peer pressure, society, social media and life. Nevertheless, God has used his word to let every believer know that simply because you believe and follow God's command, he has given you everything you will need for you and your family to experience Heaven's best.

While parents must remember how great their God has been in their lives, it must be coupled with awareness of the call and authority God has placed within them to effectively keep the holy fire burning for the next generation.

Revelation 1:6 King James Version And hath made us kings and priests unto God and his Father; to him be glory and dominion for ever and ever. Amen.

It is also important for parents to embrace their authority to equip their child. John is saying that because you believe in the finished work of the cross you have been granted access to operate as both a king and a priest. You are not a layperson, and you do not have to wait for someone to operate on your behalf. Because of the blood of Jesus, every believer has been authorized as a king and priest unto God. While believers of Christ should function in the authority of both, a king and priest, many believers feel this is only reserved for the elect or elite in the body. This simply is not true. This chapter of revelation is written for all of God's servants, so every parent is qualified to serve as a king and priest in their home with the goal of equipping their child in destiny. Still, let's briefly examine what each role looks like:

- A king takes authority
- A priest teaches and covers (as in prayers and giving sacrifices)

While the functions are definitive, as with all kings and priests, how each person operates in their role may look different. This is due to the differing gifts and abilities God has given. Consider how different Jesus' disciples were. They were all called to the same role of discipleship but because of their different spiritual DNA and personalities, how they functioned in this same role looked different. It is appropriate for each family to look different and no way of training your child is inferior if it agrees with God's vision for training children in destiny. God never mentioned perfect confidence being required to train children, all he asks for is obedience in what he instructs. It is time for parents to know that there is a call for them, and that God has given them everything they need to minister in their first place of ministry which is in the home. The destiny of each child is empowered by parents taking their role and authority in their house by faith.

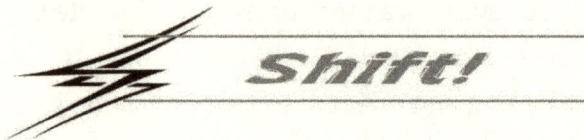

Shift!

Divine Training Protocols for Our Youth

God is sovereign so that he could use anyone he wanted to use to complete his assignment in the earth; yet, he consistently chose to use young people. He used his ministers to share an explicit message to young people.

1Timothy 4:12 Don't let anyone look down on you because you are young, but set an example for the believers in speech, in conduct, in love, in faith and in purity.

Although God is sovereign, he is still a God of order. Throughout the scripture and history, there is a pattern of using youth as agents of change. There were many people under the age of 30 that were change agents in the body of Christ.

> **(I) Identity** - The identity of the youth was revealed
>
> **(V) Vision** - God's plan or agenda for the youth was revealed
>
> **(T) Training** - Divine training occurred

In studying the agents of change in the bible, vision and identity could either be shared simultaneously or as more of a linear experience. Nevertheless, both components were the prerequisite to divine training taking place. Let's walk through how this looked for several young change agents in the bible. As parents, this gives understanding of what is important to seek the Lord for in prayer prior to conceiving, after conceiving a child, and when raising a child of God. God may not desire to wait until later to use children if parents make room for him to use them from the womb.

John the Baptist - The instructions of his training are recorded in *Luke 1:13-17.*

Luke 1:13-17 New International Bible But the angel said to him: "Do not be afraid, Zechariah; your prayer has been heard. Your wife Elizabeth will bear you a son, and you are to call him John. He will be a joy and delight to you, and many will rejoice because of his birth, for he will be great in the sight of the Lord. He is never to take wine or other fermented drink, and he will be filled with the Holy Spirit even before he is born. He will bring back many of the people of Israel to the Lord their God. And he will go on before the Lord, in the spirit and power of Elijah, to turn the hearts of the parents to their children and the disobedient to the wisdom of the righteous—to make ready a people prepared for the Lord."

Key Points:
Identity (verse 13-14): His identity was revealed in the womb. A son named John who will be a joy and delight to you, and many will rejoice because of his birth.
Vision (verse 16-17): God's vision was for John to bring many of the people to the Lord and go on before the Lord, in the spirit and power of Elijah, to make ready a people prepared for the Lord.
Training (verse 15 and beyond in life): John was never to take wine or other fermented drink and to be filled with the Holy Spirit before he was born. John even recognized and responded to Jesus in the womb in *Luke 1:41.*

Samson – At times, God's instructions will not be long and drawn out. His initial instructions for Samson's training was very succinct. The instructions of his training is in *Judges 13:4-6.*

Judges 13:4-6 New International Bible Now see to it that you drink no wine or other fermented drink and that you do not eat anything unclean. You will become pregnant and have a son whose head is never to be touched by a razor because the boy is to be a Nazarite, dedicated to God from the womb. He will take the lead in delivering Israel from the hands of the Philistines." Then the woman went to her husband and told him, "A man of God came to me. He looked like an angel of God, very awesome. I didn't ask him where he came from, and he didn't tell me his name.

Key points:
Identity (verse 5): His identity was revealed in the womb- A Nazarite, dedicated to God from the womb.
Vision (verse 5): God's vision was for Samson to take the lead in delivering Israel from the hands of the Philistines.
Training (verse 4-5): God's vision was that his mom drank no wine or other fermented drink and did not eat anything clean. Samson's hair was never to be touched by a razor because he was to be a Nazarite.

Esther - Training for this queen came after birth, yet in her youth. Esther was trained by a godly parent figure, in lieu of her parents' death. The instructions for her training are cited in *Esther 4:10- 17.*

Esther 4:10-17 New International Bible Then she instructed him to say to Mordecai, "All the king's officials and the people of the royal provinces know that for any man or woman who approaches the king in the inner court without being summoned the king has but one law: that they be put to death unless the king extends the gold scepter to them and spares their lives. But thirty days have passed since I was called to go to the king."

When Esther's words were reported to Mordecai, he sent back this answer: "Do not think that because you are in the king's house you alone of all the Jews will escape. For if you remain silent at this time, relief and deliverance for the Jews will arise from another place, but you and your father's family will perish. And who knows but that you have come to your royal position for such a time as this?"

Then Esther sent this reply to Mordecai: "Go, gather together all the Jews who are in Susa, and fast for me. Do not eat or drink for three days, night or day. I and my attendants will fast as you do. When this is done, I will go to the king, even though it is against the law. And if I perish, I perish." So Mordecai went away and carried out all of Esther's instructions.

Key points:
Identity (verse 13): She was a queen, but first a Jew
Vision (verse 14): God's vision was for Esther to bring relief and deliverance for the Jews

Training (verse 10; 15-17): Esther would walk in authority of a Queen. She would approach the king without be summoned but only after calling a fast of her and her people of not eating or drinking for three days, night or day, for divine assistance. When this was done, she would go to the king.

Jeremiah - God's instructions for this mighty prophet's training is cited in *Jeremiah 1:5-17.*

"Before I formed you in the womb, I knew you, before you were born I set you apart; I appointed you as a prophet to the nations." "Alas, Sovereign LORD," I said, "I do not know how to speak; I am too young." But the LORD said to me, "Do not say, 'I am too young.' You must go to everyone I send you to and say whatever I command you. Do not be afraid of them, for I am with you and will rescue you," declares the LORD. Then the LORD reached out his hand and touched my mouth and said to me, "I have put my words in your mouth. See, today I appoint you over nations and kingdoms to uproot and tear down, to destroy and overthrow, to build and to plant."

The word of the LORD came to me: "What do you see, Jeremiah?" "I see the branch of an almond tree," I replied. The LORD said to me, "You have seen correctly, for I am watching to see that my word is fulfilled." The word of the LORD came to me again: "What do you see?" "I see a pot that is boiling," I answered. "It is tilting toward us from the north." The LORD said to me, "From the north disaster will be poured out on all who live in the land. I am about to summon all the peoples of the northern kingdoms," declares the LORD. "Their kings will come and set up their thrones in the entrance of the gates of Jerusalem; they will come against all her surrounding walls and against all the towns of Judah. I will pronounce my judgments on my people because of their wickedness in forsaking me, in burning incense to other gods and in worshiping what their hands have made. "Get yourself ready! Stand up and say to them whatever I command you. Do not be terrified by them, or I will terrify you before them.

Key points:

Identity (Verse 5): Jeremiah's identity was revealed before he was in the womb. The bible tells us that before Jeremiah was in his mother's womb God knew him and set him apart as an appointed prophet to the nations.

Vision (Verses 7- 10): God's vision for Jeremiah's life was that even though he was young he would still go to everyone God sent him to and say whatever God commanded. God would be with Jeremiah and rescue him, so he did not need to be afraid as he uprooted and tore down, destroyed and overthrew, built and planted according to God's commands.

Training (Verse 11-17): God's trained Jeremiah himself "on the job," God put his words in Jeremiah's mouth and showed him visions and directions in private before releasing him to go into the nation. God told Jeremiah to get himself ready so he could stand up and say whatever God commanded him. God gave Jeremiah an ultimatum that either he went willingly, or God would terrify him before the people. He chose to go willingly as God led him.

Jesus: Even Jesus, our savior, was trained by his mom on several occasions. From pondering who he was, to teaching him to understand authority when he left his parents to be in the temple, to performing his first miracle. If Jesus received training under his mom's authority, through the leading of the Holy Spirit, why wouldn't every child benefit from being equipped by their parent? Jesus's training can be found in several chapters. A few scriptures regarding his training is *Luke 1:28-2:51 & John 2:1-11*.

Key Points:
Identity (Luke 1:31): His identity was revealed before he was in the womb.
Vision (Luke 1:32-33): God's vision was that Jesus would be great and called the Son of the Most High. The Lord God would give him the throne of his father David, and he will reign over Jacob's descendants forever; his kingdom will never end.
Training (John 2:5-11 & Luke 2:48-51): Jesus has the divine part of his training covered, but he was also natural and needed training in this function. Jesus' mom prompted him to begin doing miracles/ministry and Jesus had to be trained in submission to his parents after leaving them as a boy. This may have been important to complete the work on the cross.

Each change agent's journey had a different vision and destiny pathway, but the critical components remained the same. Vision is imperative to keep us as a people from perishing, and wise counsel or training is important to win a war. Thus, it only seems right that God would make these keys a significant part of divine training for his sons and daughters. What a mighty God we serve! **SHIFT RIGHT NOW!**

Young Game Changers in the Bible

Destiny should be the driving force to an entire lifestyle journey with the Lord. It is a foundational concept that is innately ignited and charged when children are conceived, and if not properly cultivated or trained. can be forfeited. We see this with King Saul who was a preferred young man among the people. King Saul had great qualities from his youth. Yet King Saul lacked the standards, boundaries, and posture he needed to sustain destiny. This caused him to forfeit his rulership as king over Israel as God rejected him due to his disobedience.

1Samuel 9:2 And he had a son, whose name was Saul, a choice young man, and a goodly: and there was not among the children of Israel a goodlier person than he: from his shoulders and upward he was higher than any of the people.

In *1Samuel 15*, God gave King Saul clear instructions to kill the Amalekites and utterly destroy everything. But King Saul and the people chose to spare King Agag and keep spoils that they felt should not be destroyed. King Saul even believed that some of these spoils could be offered to God as sacrifices. But we cannot alter God's instructions, nor can we give God what we want him to have. Therefore, it repented God to make Saul king and he rejected him.

1Samuel 15:20-24 And Saul said unto Samuel, Yea, I have obeyed the voice of the LORD, and have gone the way which the LORD sent me, and have brought Agag the king of Amalek, and have utterly destroyed the Amalekites. But the people took of the spoil, sheep and oxen, the chief of the things which should have been utterly destroyed, to sacrifice unto the LORD thy God in Gilgal. And Samuel said, Hath the LORD as great delight in burnt offerings and sacrifices, as in obeying the voice of the LORD? Behold, to obey is better than sacrifice, and to hearken than the fat of rams. For rebellion is as the sin of witchcraft, and stubbornness is as iniquity and idolatry. Because thou hast rejected the word of the LORD, he hath also rejected thee from being king. And Saul said unto Samuel, I have sinned: for I have transgressed the commandment of the LORD, and thy words: because I feared the people, and obeyed their voice.

Though Kingdom Saul did not completely fulfill his destiny in the manner God required, there are many other cases where young people were willing to serve God and experience God's kingdom on earth as it is in heaven. God's hand is on youth as they are indeed his game changers.

1John 2:14 New International Bible *I write to you, dear children, because you know the Father. I write to you, fathers, because you know him who is from the beginning. I write to you, young men, because you are strong, and the word of God lives in you, and you have overcome the evil one.*

Matthew 19:14 New International Bible *Jesus said, "Let the little children come to me, and do not hinder them, for the kingdom of heaven belongs to such as these.*

The Bible entails a host of examples where people under thirty operate as agents of change for his glory. Since there is nothing new under the sun, we should expect to see the same type of radical partnerships of young people and God today. Let's explore some young game changers that partnered with God to facilitate miracles and changes lives on heaven's behalf.

Josiah

2Chronicles 34:1-2 New International Bible Josiah was eight years old when he became king, and he reigned in Jerusalem thirty-one years. He did what was right in the eyes of the LORD and followed the ways of his father David, not turning aside to the right or to the left.

Key Considerations:

The Bible tells us Josiah was eight years old when he began his reign. His father David was a good role model for him regarding covenanting and journey with God as the word says he took after his father and walked in destiny alignment with the Lord.

Hezekiah

2Chronicles 29:1 New International Bible Hezekiah was twenty-five years old when he became king, and he reigned in Jerusalem twenty-nine years. His mother's name was Abijah daughter of Zechariah.

Key Considerations:

The Bible tells us Hezekiah was twenty-five years old when he began his reign for twenty nine years as king. When reading the story of Hezekiah, we will find that he purified and repaired God's temple, purged its idols, tore down high places, and reformed the priesthood. Though his father was wicked, he honored and followed God, and therefore prospered. Later in his reign, King Hezekiah became ill during a time of reigning and set his face to the Lord, prayed and was given fifteen more years of life.

2Kings 20:5-7 Turn again, and tell Hezekiah the captain of my people, Thus saith the LORD, the God of David thy father, I have heard thy prayer, I have seen thy tears: behold, I will heal thee: on the third day thou shalt go up unto the house of the LORD. And I will add unto thy days fifteen years; and I will deliver thee and this city out of the hand of the king of Assyria; and I will defend this city for mine own sake, and for my servant David's sake. And Isaiah said, Take a lump of figs. And they took and laid it on the boil, and he recovered.

Samuel

1Samuel 1:9-11 So Hannah rose up after they had eaten in Shiloh, and after they had drunk. Now Eli the priest sat upon a seat by a post of the temple of the LORD. And she was in bitterness of soul, and prayed unto the LORD, and wept sore. And she vowed a vow, and said, O LORD of hosts, if thou wilt indeed look on the affliction of thine handmaid, and remember me, and not forget thine handmaid, but wilt give unto thine handmaid a man child, then I will give him unto the LORD all the days of his life, and there shall no razor come upon his head.

Verse 16-17 Count not thine handmaid for a daughter of Belial: for out of the abundance of my complaint and grief have I spoken hitherto. Then Eli answered and said, Go in peace: and the God of Israel grant thee thy petition that thou hast asked of him.

1Samuel 2:18-19 *But Samuel ministered before the LORD, being a child, girded with a linen ephod. Moreover his mother made him a little coat, and brought it to him from year to year, when she came up with her husband to offer the yearly sacrifice.*

1Samuel 3:1 New International Bible *The boy Samuel ministered before the LORD under Eli. In those days the word of the LORD was rare; there were not many visions.*

1Samuel 3:7-11 *Now Samuel did not yet know the LORD, neither was the word of the LORD yet revealed unto him. And the LORD called Samuel again the third time. And he arose and went to Eli, and said, Here am I; for thou didst call me. And Eli perceived that the LORD had called the child. Therefore Eli said unto Samuel, Go, lie down: and it shall be, if he call thee, that thou shalt say, Speak, LORD; for thy servant heareth. So Samuel went and lay down in his place. And the LORD came, and stood, and called as at other times, Samuel, Samuel. Then Samuel answered, Speak; for thy servant heareth. And the LORD said to Samuel, Behold, I will do a thing in Israel, at which both the ears of every one that heareth it shall tingle.*

Key Considerations:
Samuel's mom vowed to dedicate Samuel from the womb. As God granted her wish to have a baby, she followed through on her vow. Once weaned, she took Samuel to the temple and he served the Lord from that day forward. Samuel actually lived in destiny ministering inside the presence of the Lord. His destiny

was cultivated by serving and living inside the temple where God's presence resided. He was used to God's presence but not his voice. It was Eli, the priest, who helped him to recognize God's voice. This where he learned to commune with God, hear God's voice, and become the key prophetic voice of God in a day and time where God's voice was rare.

Boy with Two Fish and Five Loaves

John 6:9 New International Bible Here is a boy with five small barley loaves and two small fish, but how far will they go among so many.

Key Considerations:
The boy's name was not mentioned; however, God chose to point out that it was a young boy who was involved in a mighty move of God. It was something as ordinary as a boy's lunch that would be the foundation of a miracle that has been shared for over two thousand years. It was not typical for Jesus to forcibly take things from people to facilitate a miracle; they had to be willing participants. Therefore, we can celebrate that this boy was willing to be selfless in sharing his food with the disciples for a greater cause. It was this boy's selfless act that teaches young and old believers alike that no small gesture goes unnoticed with God.

Naaman's Servant Girl

2Kings 5:2-3 New International Bible *Now bands of raiders from Aram had gone out and had taken captive a young girl from Israel, and she served Naaman's wife. She said to her mistress, "If only my master would see the prophet who is in Samaria! He would cure him of his leprosy.*

Key Considerations:

This young girl was taken from her home and caused to be a servant to Naaman's wife; however, even in her place of bondage she was determined to share the power of God. This young girl is an inspiration to all believers that even in our uncomfortable places or moments we have a responsibility and privilege to share the power of God with unbelievers. The girl was not forceful, but she used one respectful suggestion to reveal the living God those in authority over her. The girl suggested to her mistress that her husband, Naaman, go visit a prophet to be healed of his sickness. Naaman, a valiant but leprous soldier, received approval to go to Samaria to see Elijah the prophet for healing and went immediately. Initially, Naaman did not heed to the words of the prophet; however, his servant encouraged him to follow the directions of Elijah. Once Naaman was obedient to Elijah's instructions he was completely healed and persuaded of the one true and living God. The suggestion of this one girl caused her leaders, and those traveling with him, to personally encounter God. From this one girl's suggestion came a man's belief and repentance for bowing to another God.

David

1Samuel 16:12 New International Bible There is still the youngest," Jesse answered. "He is tending the sheep."

Number 1:3 New International Bible You and Aaron are to count according to their divisions all the men in Israel who are twenty years old or more and able to serve in the army.

1 Samuel 17:33 New International Bible Saul replied, "You are not able to go out against this Philistine and fight him; you are only a young man, and he has been a warrior form his youth."

Key Considerations:
David is known in the Bible for doing great things as king; however, before he came to this prestigious position he was almost overlooked because of his youth. Samuel came to anoint the next king of Israel and was led to Jesse's house. Jesse was David's father. Samuel had a ceremony and met seven of Jesse's sons to anoint them; however, God shared that none of David's brothers were God's chosen man for king. David was the youngest son, so he was left out of the ceremony while he tended the sheep as the youngest male. Nevertheless, Samuel made everyone wait for David to come back so that he could anoint him as king of Israel. However, even after he was anointed, David was not released to take over Israel, so he still remained at his father's house. He continued to tend the sheep while his older brothers went to serve the standing King, Saul, in the war. It was during this time that David's breakthrough moment came as followed his father's instructions to bring food to his brothers before battle. It was at this appointed time that

he met and defeated Goliath. What many people do not know is that David was not old enough to fight in the war. David was under the age 20 at the time he fought Goliath. We know this because according to *Numbers 1:3* only men over the age of 20 could serve in the army. In addition, in *1 Samuel 17:33,* Saul called David only a young boy opposed to Goliath who had served in war since his youth. Even though David was the youngest and counted out in both situations he was still used by God to show that God does not look on the outward appearances to use people; he looks at the heart. David's heart for God showed that even the youngest man or woman can save a nation in the name of the Lord.

Some of the 12 Disciples:

Matthew 17:24-27 New International Bible After Jesus and his disciples arrived in Capernaum, the collectors of the two-drachma temple tax came to Peter and asked, "Doesn't your teacher pay the temple tax?" "Yes, he does," he replied. When Peter came into the house, Jesus was the first to speak. "What do you think, Simon?" he asked. "From whom do the kings of the earth collect duty and taxes—from their own children or from others?" "From others," Peter answered. "Then the children are exempt," Jesus said to him. "But so that we may not cause offense, go to the lake and throw out your line. Take the first fish you catch; open its mouth and you will find a four-drachma coin. Take it and give it to them for my tax and yours."

Key Considerations:
According to Matthew 17:24-27 the disciples who were with Jesus, were under twenty, except Peter and himself. This scripture shares that at the very least Peter, James, and John were with Jesus, yet he only paid temple tax for himself and Peter. This is important to note because Exodus 30:13-16 instructs the people that only those twenty years and older must pay half a shekel in temple tax. Jesus paid one shekel which means he paid for only two people showing that two people, including himself, were twenty years or older. Jesus did not come to abolish the law, so this exchange creates an understanding that some of the disciples, at least James and John, were under twenty years old and young game changers in the bible. In addition, according to theologians and Hebrew culture, males under twenty were chosen by their rabbi while in the tradesmen timeframe of their lives, just as Jesus' disciples were. The bible speaks to how the twelve disciples were conducting their tradesmen duties when Jesus called them to follow him. While this understanding is based on theological and Hebrew study, historically, the pharisee's criticized everything contrary to Jewish customs that Jesus did; however, they never once questioned how Jesus picked his disciples. Furthermore, in *Matthew 20:20-28,* James and John's mother vouched for them with Jesus. This was a conversation that was typically held with a Rabbi in the Jewish culture while a male was younger and still within their mother's household. This lack of criticism from the pharisees and persuasion from a mother work together to insinuate that Jesus took a traditional route to this decision and that his disciples were indeed under twenty years old when they were called to follow and serve.

Esther

Esther 2:2 **New International Version** *Then the king's personal attendants proposed, Let a search be made for beautiful young virgins for the king.*

Key Considerations:
Esther was taken in by her uncle, Mordecai, and was a young virgin in the land. In the biblical timeframe young women were married in their teens, as it was also a financial transaction between families. According to theologians and Hebraic culture, Esther was around fourteen or fifteen years old when she became queen, particularly in looking at how she is described as a beautiful young virgin in the bible.

Jeremiah

Jeremiah 1:6-7 New International Version *"Alas, Sovereign LORD," I said, "I do not know how to speak; I am too young." But the LORD said to me, "Do not say, 'I am too young.'*

Key Considerations:
Jeremiah went on to become known as the "weeping prophet," but his story as a prophet did not start so boldly. Theologians suggest that Jeremiah was about 17 when God called him. While we do not know Jeremiah's exact age when he was called to serve as a prophet, we do know that Jeremiah and God had an explicit conversation about his youth being an obstacle in service. Jeremiah's father was a priest of God; however, Jeremiah was not yet old or bold enough to operate as a

mouthpiece of God. Yet, one encounter with the true and living God shifted his level of boldness and caused him to cry loud and spare not for the people of God to return to the Lord. Jeremiah was a great candidate to show us that a young person's confidence doesn't have to be great to obey God. They just need faith that God will be with them.

Although this is not an exhaustive list of all young game changers it gives a clear indication that God intends to use young people to fulfill his purposes in the earth. Therefore, destiny is not something to be attained at a later age, but rather in each present moment to fulfill kingdom assignments early. The determining factors for kingdom partnerships remain a person's willingness, obedience, and training which are all independent to one's age.

The Blessed Weapons of Children

The Bible is very clear that while living as a child of God is a blessed life, it is not a guarantee to avoid troubles or struggles. This fact stands for young and older believers. In fact, God is so faithful to give his children a clear understanding that there is a very real enemy who comes to take what Jesus has worked to give us.

John 10:10 New International Bible The thief comes only to steal and kill and destroy; I have come that they may have life and have it to the full.

To enjoy the full life Jesus came to give us, it is imperative that the people of God are aware of their authority, as well as the weapons that have been granted to protect what has rightfully been given to them by the blood of Jesus.

Ephesians 6:17 New International Bible Take the helmet of salvation and the sword of the Spirit, which is the word of God.

2Corinthians: 10:4 New International Bible The weapons we fight with are not the weapons of the world. On the contrary, they have divine power to demolish strongholds.

2Corinthians 10:4 is a game changer because many Christians are well versed with the offensive weapon of the sword, which is the word of God; however, 2 Corinthians 10:4 uses a very small but important word that gives more insight into the divine arsenal of heaven.

WEAPONS (plural) This tells us that there is more than one weapon in the spirit realm, so the question is what other weapons do we have access to?

ARROWS

Psalm 91:5 New International Bible *You will not fear the terror of night, nor the <u>arrow</u> that flies by day.*

Psalm 127:4 New International Bible *Like <u>arrows</u> in the hands of a warrior are children born in one's youth.*

This is such an important fact because different fights require different weapons. Swords are for face to face battle. Arrows are effective for long distance warfare. When David went to fight Goliath, he only had his slingshot, but Goliath thought he was prepared for any situation since he had both a sword and spear with him.

As people of God we must be aware of our enemy's tactics. The enemy does not always fight face to face. Sometimes he goes through distance, or bloodlines, so there needs to be an arrow or bloodline breaker that uses wisdom to identify the target and hit it spot on with God's authority which cuts off the illegal activity of the enemy in bloodlines. Children are heaven's secret weapons. They are indeed as arrows in the hands of their parents because when equipped for destiny they can do greater works for God's kingdom than their parents.

Unfortunately, this is a revelation that has not been understood by many believers so families move through religious routines while waiting, hoping, and praying that children grow up and not go astray. Yet, it is in this same "waiting" time that God wants to use children as arrows to break up fallow ground in bloodlines because, just like David, they appear to be underdogs but with training and heaven's backing they have the ability to conquer every bullying spirit that has tormented families for generations.

This waiting period of children to grow is precisely why families see the same behaviors, issues, personalities, and mindset cycle through generations. The people of God have only been using swords when arrows have been a very viable and deadly weapon for use. Now that it is known, it is time to wake up the weapons that have been lying dormant in our homes. Arrows go further than where the warrior stands who is releasing them and this same concept applies when parents train and release their children for God's glory. Young people are called because they are strong and can strike faster & more precisely than their parents did. It is not an insult to parents, but just a manifestation of the promise of God. We are called to go from glory to glory. If we do not release children as arrows the work of the lineage will cycle or start over again and that is not the plan of God for his people. We as a body of believers should look like a move from glory to glory.

2Corinthians 3:18 New International Bible But we all, with open face beholding as in a glass the glory of the Lord, are changed into the same image from glory to glory, even as by the Spirit of the Lord.

Jesus was also the epitome of using young people as arrows when he shared the concept that those coming after him will do greater works than he did on the earth.

John 14:12 New International Bible Very truly I tell you, whoever believes in me will do the works I have been doing, and they will do even greater things than these, because I am going to the Father.

While this is a spiritual aspect, there are also many natural examples of this concept in the bible. Let's review a handful of parents that successfully trained and released their natural or spiritual child, who then took the assignment of their parent and went further to advance God's kingdom.

- Elijah (8 miracles) -> Elisha (16 miracles)
- Hannah (activated 1 prophet) -> Samuel (activated many leaders)
- Jesse (made 1 leader) -> David (made a kingdom lineage)
- David (prepared God's temple) -> Solomon (completed the temple)
- Joseph (saved his son) -> Jesus (saved the world

Shift!

Negating the Blessings of Children

Child Abuse
Child abuse negates the blessing of children and the inheritance of who they are in our lives and family lineage. Children are guiltless and innocent in God's eyes. To abuse them – to provoke them to anger and trauma – is an abomination in God's eyes a incite his judgment.

Ephesians 6:4 And, ye fathers, provoke not your children to wrath: but bring them up in the nurture and admonition of the Lord.

Mark 9:42 And whosoever shall offend one of [these] little ones that believe in me, it is better for him that a millstone were hanged about his neck, and he were cast into the sea.

Exodus 21:22 If men strive, and hurt a woman with child, so that her fruit depart [from her], and yet no mischief follow: he shall be surely punished, according as the woman's husband will lay upon him; and he shall pay as the judges [determine].

Exodus 23:7 Keep thee far from a false matter; and the innocent and righteous slay thou not: for I will not justify the wicked.

Deuteronomy 2:25 Cursed be he that taketh reward to slay an innocent person. And all the people shall say, Amen.

Colossians 3:21 Fathers, provoke not your children [to anger], lest they be discouraged.

According to childhelp.org, child abuse is defined is *"when a parent or caregiver, whether through action or failing to act, causes injury, death, emotional harm or risk of serious harm to a child. There are many forms of child maltreatment, including neglect, physical abuse, sexual abuse, exploitation and emotional abuse."*

Depending on the type of abuse, it can strip children of their identity and cause them to be stunted in their spiritual, physical, and natural growth. Abuse can cause them to develop a complex and live on to reinforce generational cycles of abuse and brokenness.

Abuse often can even strip children from their families. Children who are placed in the foster care system are then dependent on strangers to define who they are and what their identity is, when truly they were born into those specific family lines for a reason. Abuse can kill the kingdom heir – the bloodline breaker - before they ever take their place in restoring the blessings of the Lord back into the family. Instead of focusing on identity development and destiny, abused children spend their lives trying to get basic needs of love, safety, and acceptance met. It is a destiny thief and killer.

Next to aborting one's destiny, abusing, misusing, trafficking, and neglecting a child's destiny can stifle them to the point where they do not even desire God's blueprint but are stuck in a lifelong cycle of trauma and crisis. Abuse and trauma open the door to a gateway to other destiny killing spirits where the child was once fighting to overcome abuse and healing are now more susceptible to all of these other destiny killing spirits attached to their trauma. The spirits of rejection, abandonment, fear, inadequacy, etc., all work together to dismantle the child's identity before they can develop into destiny.

Children who were subjected to emotional, physical, or sexual abuse, are more likely to suffer from re-victimization as adults, physical health problems, mental health challenges, suicidal ideations, drug and alcohol addiction, obesity and eating disorders, homelessness, becoming generational abusers, criminal & high risk behavior, and the list goes on.

Abortion
Abortion is defined as a safe and legal way to end pregnancy. This is murder as in order to end pregnancy, you must end a life.

- Medication Abortion is known as the abortion pill. It is called, *"Plan B."* It keeps the sperm from connecting to the egg.

- Abortions tend to be conducted as if it is a choice to deal with unwanted pregnancy, management family size, financial hardship due to increased family members in the home, or population control.

People have abortion for various reasons:

- Some were not planning to be pregnant, and do not want to keep the baby they have created.

- Some may experience raped, molestation, trafficked, and thus do not want to keep the baby under these circumstances.
- Some are under eighteen; they and/or their caregivers are not ready for them to care for a baby.
- Some unmarried women have abortions to avoid shame and reproach of having sex and a baby out of wedlock, hardship that comes with not being able to financial care for a child, not being ready to be a parent, not having a sufficient partner to help care for the baby.
- Some women are force to have an abortion by their partners or those that impregnate them.
- Some are told their health is at risk if they follow through with giving birth.
- Some are told the baby will be born dead, deformed, mentally challenged if they follow through with giving birth.
- Some become pregnant for the purposes of sacrificing the baby to an idol god.
- Planned Parenthood is federal program that provides health services in the following areas: STD testing and treatment, birth control, well-woman exams, cancer screening and prevention, abortion, hormone therapy, infertility services, and general health care. Plan Parenthood Centers are stationed in communities, especially low-income communities. They have created a system and culture of abortion as necessary or appropriate for those that are already poverty stricken, living in low income home, or part of the Medicaid system.

- Believe it or not some abortion clinics are really witchcraft cult groups. After they extract the baby from the woman and the woman leaves the clinic, they do rituals regarding the baby. They drink the blood that was drained from the procedure and the baby, then offer the baby up as a sacrifice to an idol god.

Sometimes people can perform illegal abortions:

- They may take substances, put items inside of themselves, abuse their stomachs, so they can lose the baby.
- They may go to someone who is not a legalized doctor and allow this person to perform an abortion upon them.
- They may go to a witchcraft doctor or high priest who will cast a spell on them or perform some type of ritual or procedure on them, so they can miscarry the baby.
- They may speak curses over themselves and these words, cause the baby to miscarry.

Abort73.com reports the following Annual Abortion Statistics:
- ➢ Based on available state-level data, approximately 876,000 abortions took place in the United States in 2018.
- ➢ According to the Guttmacher Institute, an estimated 862,320 abortions took place in the United States in 2017—down from 926,240 in 2014.
- ➢ Based on available state-level data, approximately 890,000 abortions took place in the United States in

2016—down from approximately 913,000 abortions in 2015.

➤ In 2017, approximately 18% of U.S. pregnancies (excluding spontaneous miscarriages) ended in abortion.

➤ According to the United Nations' 2013 report, only nine countries in the world have a higher reported abortion rate than the United States. They are: Bulgaria, Cuba, Estonia, Georgia, Kazakhstan, Romania, Russia, Sweden, and Ukraine.

➤ *Though the UN lists China's official abortion rate at 19.2, China's actual abortion rate is likely much higher. According to China's 2010 census, there were approximately 310 million women of reproductive age in the country. An estimated 13-23 million abortions happen annually in China, resulting in an adjusted abortion rate of 41.9-74.2. The abortion rate is the number of abortions per 1,000 women aged 15-44.

➤ In 2017, the highest percentage of pregnancies were aborted in the District of Columbia (37%), New Jersey (32%), and New York (31%). The lowest percentage of pregnancies were aborted in Idaho (5%), South Dakota (4%), and Wyoming (2%). (AGI abortion data + CDC birth data).

➤ In 2016, approximately 34% of all pregnancies in New York City (excluding spontaneous miscarriages) ended in abortion (CDC).

➤ The annual number of legal induced abortions in the United States doubled between 1973 and 1979 and peaked in 1990 (CDC).

- From 2015 to 2016, the number and rate2 of reported abortions decreased by 2%. The abortion ratio3 decreased by 1% (CDC).
- More than 60 million legal abortions have occurred in the United States since 1973.

These numbers should be alarming. Even now we repent Lord from every way we have not regarded abortions as murder. We repent for not understanding that this is a killing of children and a disregard of a life. Forgive us Lord for this and especially forgive us if we are believers who have made abortion appear appropriate and any way, we have suggested abortions as an option to the people you have granted to our hands.

Sex Trafficking

Sex trafficking and child labor is a displacement of children from the alignment and will of God. It is the action or practice of illegally transporting children from one country or area to another, typically for the purposes of forced labor, marriage, prostitution, sexual exploitation and organ removal. When a child is exploited, they are use or utilized for profit or someone's else's gain, needs or pleasure.

The International Labor Organization (ILO) estimates that 1.2 million children are trafficked each year. This number is increasing at alarming rates. Most sex trafficking victims are women and girls, though men, boys, trans, intersex and nonbinary individuals can be victims as well. According to the International Labor Organization report, more than 70% of sex trafficking victims were located in Asia and the Pacific, compared with 14% in Europe and Central Asia and 4% in the Americas.

In illicit massage parlors in the U.S., the vast majority of reported trafficking victims are from China, with a notable number from the Fujian province in southeastern China. South Korea forms the second highest group.

As we consider this topic, we can explore the possibility that abortion and sex trafficking in the natural realm is the spirit of Molech running rampant in our society.

Leviticus 18:21 *And thou shalt not let any of thy seed pass through the fire to Molech, neither shalt thou profane the name of thy God: I am the LORD.*

2Kings 16:3 *But he walked in the way of the kings of Israel; indeed he made his son pass through the fire, according to the abominations of the nations whom the LORD had cast out from before the children of Israel.*

Ezekiel 23:36-39 *The Lord said moreover unto me; Son of man, wilt thou judge Aholah and Aholibah? yea, declare unto them their abominations; That they have committed adultery, and blood is in their hands, and with their idols have they committed adultery, and have also caused their sons, whom they bare unto me, to pass for them through the fire, to devour them. Moreover this they have done unto me: they have defiled my sanctuary in the same day, and have profaned my sabbaths. For when they had slain their children to their idols, then they came the same* *day into my sanctuary to profane it; and, lo, thus have they done in the midst of mine house.*

When the people offered sacrifices to their idol god – Molech - they would put the child in the fire as a sacrifice of purification. How did they see this as a sacrifice of purification exceeds anything most of us can grasp, but this is how idolatry will twist your thinking into believing right is wrong and wrong is right. And in this case, having some operating in such a wretched evil act and them thinking it is benefiting their lives and is an honor to a demon god.

When children are trafficked, they are sacrificed as if their lives and destinies have no value. They are no more than a commodity, objects, slaves, labor. Their innocence, identity, and childhood is stolen at the expense of someone's else's perversion, sin, or transgression.

Some parents are selling their children into trafficking for money. The child is sold all together or is someone's slave while money is sent to their parents to help pay bills. All types of things happen to these children as they are stripped of their innocence, childhood, and identity for the sake of their family. Some parents who have lots of children will sell their children into child labor or sex trafficking, so they do not have to care for them. If parents and traffickers regarded the value for life, and understood godly purpose, and had revelation that children destined for greatness from the womb, these activities world not be as prevalent. We must start advocating for the godly value of our children. We must change the mindset of how they are viewed so that they will be regarded and even begin to live their destiny and purpose from the womb.

Our Children Will Serve False Gods

2Chronicles 33:1-8 Manasseh was twelve years old when he began to reign, and he reigned fifty and five years in Jerusalem: But did that which was evil in the sight of the Lord, like unto the abominations of the heathen, whom the Lord had cast out before the children of Israel. For he built again the high places which Hezekiah his father had broken down, and he reared up altars for Baalim, and made groves, and worshipped all the host of heaven, and served them. Also he built altars in the house of the Lord, whereof the Lord had said, In Jerusalem shall my name be for ever.

And he built altars for all the host of heaven in the two courts of the house of the Lord. And he caused his children to pass through the fire in the valley of the son of Hinnom: also he observed times, and used enchantments, and used witchcraft, and dealt with a familiar spirit, and with wizards: he wrought much evil in the sight of the Lord, to provoke him to anger. And he set a carved image, the idol which he had made, in the house of God, of which God had said to David and to Solomon his son, In this house, and in Jerusalem, which I have chosen before all the tribes of Israel, will I put my name for ever.

When children are not cultivated in destiny, they can end up walking in their calling, but using their purpose for evil. In this passage of scripture, we see Manasseh begin to reign as king at age 12. But he did not know the Lord. He was not cultivated in godly destiny. He therefore reigned 55 years in Jerusalem while leading the people in idolatry. He rebuilt high places that were torn down. He had no fear or reverence for the Lord as he built high place inside the house of the Lord. He sacrificed his children and engaged in all types of idolatrous witchcraft practices.

Manasseh was basically a childhood warlock who groomed his nation to be witches and warlocks. We have a lot of childhood witches and warlocks in society today. Some are taught by their parents and others ignorantly become witches and warlocks through the culture trends released in society. We have a lot of children engaging in idolatrous witchcraft practices today because they are not cultivated in destiny, neither are they taught to serve the Lord. They are exposed to witchcraft at an early age through cartoons, TV shows and movies, books, social media, peers, etc. Prayer has been taken out of school, while witchcraft has crept into the school through yoga and other meditation new age practices that are perceived as harmless. Many parents do not attend church or serve God themselves. Many children have been given more leeway by parents to dictate what is good for them so many children do not attend church even if their parents go. Children are dictating what type of clothing is appropriate for them, what peer group is best for them, what sex and gender they want to be, etc. Laws are being put in place to allow children to make these choices, thus further stripping the voice and the rights of parents to effectively govern their households. A lack of true God identity is causing children to be depressed and suicidal if they are not allowed to change their sex and/or gender. Fears of losing children to mental illness and/or death further binds their hands of parents and law makers. As a result, definitions like the ones below are being institutionalize to help re-identify children and people who want to be classified in a different sex or gender other than the one they one born as.

- **Gender Confusion** - Individual's feeling of not identifying with his or her assigned gender.
- **Neutral Genealogy** - Not wanting to be defined by a specific gender, even the gender one was born in.
- **Gender Genocide** - systematic killing of the origin of gender that specifically defines and separates us as male and female.

The culture and gender epidemic we are experiencing with children wanting to change their sex and people not wanting to be identified by gender, derives from a lack of governing:

- God's standard of him and his biblical principles being the foundation of our lives and families, where his ordained will, purpose, and destinies for our lives is active and flourishing all down through our generations.
- God's innate purpose for procreation.
- God's innate purpose for family.
- The woman's honor and position as a birther - creator - a womb bearer.
- The man's honor as head and carrier of God's family legacy in the earth.
- Our seed and egg even before procreation.
- The womb as children are incubated during pregnancy.

- DNA and personality interruptions and interferences due to what is being put into a child's body through foods, beverages, medicines, medical procedures, and vaccinations.

No one in the bible ever created themselves. God is the author of all creation. To decide you are going to change your identity is to decide that you are your own God and creator. The bible warns us of this.

Romans 1:21-27 Because that, when they knew God, they glorified him not as God, neither were thankful; but became vain in their imaginations, and their foolish heart was darkened. Professing themselves to be wise, they became fools, And changed the glory of the uncorruptible God into an image made like to corruptible man, and to birds, and fourfooted beasts, and creeping things.

Wherefore God also gave them up to uncleanness through the lusts of their own hearts, to dishonor their own bodies between themselves: Who changed the truth of God into a lie, and worshipped and served the creature more than the Creator, who is blessed for ever. Amen. For this cause God gave them up unto vile affections: for even their women did change the natural use into that which is against nature: And likewise also the men, leaving the natural use of the woman, burned in their lust one toward another; men with men working that which is unseemly, and receiving in themselves that recompense of their error which was meet.

When our households do not worship and serve God, and when we and our children are not cultivated in God identity and his purpose for our lives, we risk being influenced by the demonic realm, culture and trends, the world's system, generational curses and propensities, and by our ideology of what we believe is right or wrong. For a time, God convicts us and tries to turn us back to him. But the more we succumb to vain imaginations, God turns us over to serve what we have created. We think it's right because we lack conviction. We do not realize that ww have become reprobate.

Genesis 1:26-28 *God said, Let Us [Father, Son, and Holy Spirit] make mankind in Our image, after Our likeness, and let them have complete authority over the fish of the sea, the birds of the air, the [tame] beasts, and over all of the earth, and over everything that creeps upon the earth. So God created man in His own image, in the image and likeness of God He created him; male and female He created them. And God blessed them and said to them, Be fruitful, multiply, and fill the earth, and subdue it [using all its vast resources in the service of God and man]; and have dominion over the fish of the sea, the birds of the air, and over every living creature that moves upon the earth.*

We are made in the image (physical likeness-representation of God) and likeness (spiritual likeness-act like God) - reflecting his identity and nature. Gender is part of the foundation of our identity in God. God created us this way because he is about replication, procreation, multiplication, fruitfulness, advancement and mankind being responsible and accountable over what they produce and reproduce. This is the reason he gave male and female dominion in the earth.

Dominion means to assert governmental rule and reign in every sphere of our lives. We cannot properly reign in our God ordained image and likeness when we reject our gender, as it provides a significant distinction of how we are to have dominion in the earth.

- Male - dress it and to keep - serve as a laborer, work, worship, care for, provide, be a watchman, guard, protect
- Female - help meet - help, relief, relieve, aid, assist

To reject our gender is to reject his image - the likeness to which he created us and identified us as his. To reject our gender SHIFTS us into a role of God's likeness that he did not ordain for us; we therefore cannot properly function in the earth. When we do not properly govern in the dominion of our gender, we cannot govern properly in our God ordained identity. Our God ordained identity entails who and what God uniquely created us to be and do in the earth.

As we lived through our God ordained identity, we must also govern over our seed. Our seed is what we are to produce and reproduce in the earth, particularly children. Seed also entail:

- Life and resources water - fish of the sea
- lands, regions, and airways - fouls of the air
- Animals - creepy things

When we go about living life without governing through the authority God has given us, we give way for the enemy to creep in and establish his kingdom, principles, wickedness, and strongholds in our midst. Especially in regard to our children. They are the ultimate seed that keeps life going and that carries the image, likeness and dominion of God from generation to generation.

Demonic Design

We can shape our lives and even the lives of others by our words, especially our children. This is the reason the Bible warns us to be careful with our words.

Proverbs 13:3 *He who guards his mouth preserves his life, But he who opens wide his lips shall have destruction.*

Proverbs 18:21 *Death and life are in the power of the tongue: and they that love it shall eat the fruit thereof.*

Matthew 12:37 *For by thy words thou shalt be justified, and by thy words thou shalt be condemned.*

Demonic design is when our words create, recreate, and design a thing according to our own will and desire, man's will and purpose, or the devil's will and purpose, thus destroying - releasing death - to God's original design.

We see this with parents who wanted and boy but got a girl or vice versus. In some cases, the child begins to think, mold, and shape into what their parents have spoken with their words rather than into their original design. This can also happen with children who are abused, teased, and called names. They begin to behave, act, and feel like what is being spoken.

God let us know that his thoughts and ways are not like ours. His ways are good and have an intended purpose.

Isaiah 55:8 For my thoughts are not your thoughts, neither are your ways my ways, saith the LORD.

Jeremiah 29:11 For I know the thoughts that I think toward you, saith the LORD, thoughts of peace, and not of evil, to give you an expected end.

<u>*Thoughts* is *machashebeth* in Hebrew and means:</u>
1. a contrivance, i.e. (concretely) a texture, machine, or (abstractly) intention, plan (whether bad, a plot; or good, advice)
2. cunning (work), curious work, device(-sed)
3. imagination, invented, means, purpose, thought

Psalms 40:50 Many, O LORD my God, are thy wonderful works which thou hast done, and thy thoughts which are to us-ward: they cannot be reckoned up in order unto thee: if I would declare and speak of them, they are more than can be numbered.

Our words can invent our will, thus appearing as if we designed something good or godly. Yet it is cunning, a curious work, witchcraft, a form of godliness, and a mechanism of producing our own workings in people, situations or in the earth. We must be careful what we speak, especially over our children as it can alter their identity. The child can then become confused and begin to war between what was contrived and what is the true creation of God concerning their life.

These word curses have to be repented for and broken off the child's life and identity. And depending on how long the child begin to engage in the demonic design, determines the level of deliverance they will need to root it out of their character, personality, and behavior. Though possible, it can be a lot of work for a child to do. If the demonic designed is not explained to them, and if they are not taught how to have a personal relationship with God and how his identity is the essence of their lives, they may find deliverance from an altered design wearisome. They may also feel as if they are being judged or rejected for living through the demonic design rather than God's original design. This is how depression and suicide find an entry way into a child's life who is experience this type of challenge. It will be important for the parents to have patience with the child, gently and strategically walk them through deliverance, while watching the words that they further speak over, to and about their child. As such words can SHIFT the child into rebelling against deliverance and pursuing the demonic design despite what God and their parents are speaking concerning their lives.

An example of a demonic design in the Bible is the story of Jabez. Though this design was probably not intentional, it still had an alarming impact on Jabez. Jabez's mother Penuel, birthed him in pain. She therefore named him Jabez which means, "pain, sorrow, sorrowful, grief and idol." Penuel most likely was expressing the labor she endured during birth and was referring to the curse of Eve found in Genesis 3:16. Though this was a judgment released to women due to Eve disobeying God and eating from the tree of knowledge, it was not a curse for a woman's seed to bear. Biblical names spoke meaning to the child's future, and the name Jabez predicted that the baby boy would become a man who would bring pain to others. By naming her child Jabez, Penuel inadvertently placed a curse upon her own son by naming him such a challenging name.

Genesis 3:16 *To the woman he said, "I will surely multiply your pain in childbearing; in pain you shall bring forth children. Your desire shall be contrary to your husband, but he shall rule over you."*

Sidebar Revelation: In considering Jabez's name, we can also discern that it is important to be careful what we name our children. Names have an impact on our children's lives. When spoken, the meaning of those names bellow into the atmosphere and empowers what the name means. Or what God has spoken or ordained regarding the child is unable to be awakened, because the child was not name properly to enliven what God instilled in the earth.

Isaiah 49:1-3 *Listen, O isles, unto me; and hearken, ye people, from afar; The LORD hath called me from the womb; from the bowels of my mother hath he made mention of my name. And he hath made my mouth like a sharp sword; in the shadow of his hand hath he hid me, and made me a polished shaft; in his quiver hath he hid me; And said unto me, Thou art my servant, O Israel, in whom I will be glorified.*

Okay now, back to the revelation at hand: The Bible says that Jabez was more honorable than all his brothers. This lets us know that his destiny was not one of sorrow, idolatry, and pain. The identity of God in him was one of nobility and prosperity. He obviously sought to prevail over the negativity attached to his name. His prayer was notable enough that his words interrupt a flow of genealogy in the Book of Chronicles. Jabez is proof that generational curses can be broken despite the names or nicknames assigned by family.

1Chronicles 4:9 *And Jabez was more honourable than his brethren: and his mother called his name Jabez, saying, Because I bare him with sorrow.*

We do not know his mother's intent, but surely his name reminded her of the pain she endured birthing him. To be reminded that you brought pain upon your mom was probably a daily constant reminded that Jabez dreaded. It is likely that it released sorrow and pain on his life as the very mention of his name was rooted in a memory that inflicted hardship rather than blessing. It is not too much of a stretch to imagine that the boy's name made him feel obligated to straighten up or to thankful of his life and mother as if he had some type of debt he owed her due to being a child of travail during birth. This is a debt that should not have been bestowed upon him, but the demonic design of his name, altered - SHIFTED - his identity to daily paying a debt that he did not intentionally cause, but through one word, was contrived to pay.

Verse 10 *And Jabez called on the God of Israel, saying, Oh that thou wouldest bless me indeed, and enlarge my coast, and that thine hand might be with me, and that thou wouldest keep me from evil, that it may not grieve me! And God granted him that which he requested.*

We see from this passage that Jabez recognized his God identity was not one of sorrow. He wanted and pursued God's design for his life and knew that only God could break the demonic design his mother had placed on him. Jabez sought God to be delivered of the curse of his name; God granted his request. His designed changed to that of the original intent of God for his destiny.

Parents must guard their words and even consider the intents of their hearts when naming, speaking about, and engaging their children. One word can alter their design and have them warring between God's identity and man's or the devil's identity for their lives.

Demonic Spirits That Attacks Children in Destiny

Spirits of Idolatry & Witchcraft - These spirits cause children to become idol worshipers, witches, and warlocks. They engage in blood sacrifices, vows, and covenants with their peers, do rituals to make bonds and pacts in their relationships, engage in self-inflicting cutting behaviors to numb pain or to offer sacrifices to idols and demons, do spells on people. They may learn this behavior from parents, caregivers, peers or from cartoons, TV shows, social media and the internet. Such open doors cause them to be fascinated with magic, astrology, horoscopes, wizards, witches, divination, spells, the spirit world, spirits of the dead, Halloween, pagan practices, Yoga, Karate, martial arts, Ouija boards, witchcraft games, minds craft games, blood thirst games and activities, occultism, and satanism *(Exodus 711, 12, Exodus 20:3-6, Daniel 4:7, Psalms 135:15-18, Isaiah 2:8, Ezekiel 18:14-17, Romans 120, Galatians 5:22-23, Colossians 1:15, 1John 5:21).*

Spirit of Molech - Spirit of Abortion - Wants to kill a child before they are born. Wants children to return to heaven; wants children to be offered up as sacrifices to the devil *(Psalms 82:3-4, Exodus 21:22-25, Leviticus 18:21, 1Kings 11:7, 2Kings 23:10, Ezekiel 16:21).*

Spirits of Premature Death - Wants to kill a child while in the womb or before they have had time to live and fulfill destiny *(Exodus 15:11, Exodus 12:29, Exodus 12, Luke 17-19 John 4:46-52, Luke 8:49-55, Matthew 9:23-25, Mark 5:38-43).*

Spirits of Suicide - Wants to coerce a child to take their own life. Spirit will often come as a familiar spirit that serves as a playmate, spiritual guide, and/or friend to a child. Will use unfavorable situations such as bullying, low self-esteem, lack of friends and fitting into peer groups to talk the child in feeling hopeless about life and living, while considering suicide as a coping mechanism. The challenge is that suicide is a final act. You cannot comeback from suicide as it is not a coping mechanism but murder of self *(Psalms 55:22, Jeremiah 29:11, John 10:10).*

Spirits of Sabotage - Wants a child to engage in activities and behaviors to sabotage his destiny or creates life scenarios to sabotage the progress, growth, life, and/or destiny of a child *(Judges 16).*

Spirits of Rebellion - Causes a child to rebel against parents, teachers, authority figures, and/God; the child maybe self-willed, selfish, stubborn, controlling, vengeful, vindictive, bitter, aggressive, violent, lawless; they can be unruly, anti-submissive, uncontrollable, intolerable, while resisting, rejecting or defying rules, regulations, boundaries, laws, and standards that would keep them in order, safe, and regarding the rights of organization, society, and other people. *(Proverbs 13:24, Proverbs 20:11, Proverbs 22:15, 1Samuel 15:23-25, Ephesians 6:1-3)*

Orphan Spirit - Causes parents to give up or leave a child for other parents, people, communities, society, or organizational systems to care for, nurture, raise, develop, train, and equip for life and destiny. Such experience can cause a child to feel void, wounded, rejected, unloved, devalued, disregard, unwanted, displaced in their identity, life, worth, and destiny. Child can have difficult bonding or feeling attached or connected to others or if they have a place in life. It is important for new parents and/or caregivers to understand that when they take a child in or adopt a child, they now have legal and spiritual authority over that child's life and destiny. That child SHIFTS under their care and governmental rulership and they can break generational and life curses off that child, cast demonic spirits out of them, and SHIFT them under the blessings, identity and blessings of Jesus Christ. It is therefore important for that parent or caregiver to consciously bond with adopted children and spend time praying over them, while literally and spiritually connecting them in mind, heart, soul, body, identity, to them personally, to the family, and under their covering as parents *(Exodus 2:1-10, Psalms 27:10-14)*.

Spirits of Abandonment - Causes a parent to abandon a child. Child can be left at birth or some point in their life. Such an experience can cause a child to feel deserted, unwanted, outcast, displaced, and forsaken. Child is left with wounds in their soul, heart, and identity. If not healed can battle fears of abandonment throughout life and have a difficulty attaching or trusting others due to abandonment issues *(Psalms 27:10-14)*.

Spirit of the Vagabond - Causes the life course of a child to drift or take a direction where the child is wandering, drifting, or feeling helpless about life and his or her destiny. This can happen if a parent moves around a lot while the child is growing up, if the child does not experience a stable and safe home life while growing up, if the child is orphaned, abandoned, displaced at any time in childhood. The child can have difficulty sitting still, being quiet and attentive, staying focused, or settling into a stable environment or relationship. Child can become a drifting wandering adult that is always trying to find his or her place, identity, and destiny; can have trouble committing, settling and being rooted and grounded in life, success or relationships. The spirit of vagabond ca sometimes be due to a curse *(Genesis 4:12-14, Proverbs 6:11, Psalms 109:10, Jeremiah 48:12, Acts 19:13-20)*.

Outcast Spirits - Cause children to feel like they do not fit in or belong. Child feels and believes they are always on the outskirts of peer groups and life situations or that they are not accepted or good enough for particular peer groups, organizations, activities, projects, social settings, experiences, or assignments *(Isaiah 56:7-8, Isaiah 16:3, Jeremiah 30:17, Psalms 147:2)*.

Spirits of Rejection - Creates situations that causes wounds in a child's soul so they will reject themselves, reject their identity, reject destiny, reject their lives, reject progressing healthy or successfully in life, and fear rejection from others. Many orphans, abandoned, displaced, outcast, and bullied children experience rejection. If these wounds are not healed, it opens the door for a spirit of rejection to come in and form a personality of rejection in the child. This spirit of rejection rules their identity and cause them to constantly be victimized through rejected experiences, and to victimize themselves by creating situations where they are rejecting others, rejecting truth, rejecting themselves and blaming it on others, or by experiencing rejection from people, life, and society *(Genesis 37:2-36, 2Kings 17, Hosea 4:6, Luke 9:22)*.

Spirit of Self-Hatred - Causes a child to hate themselves. They may want to be someone else other than themselves; will constantly speak negative of themselves. Deem themselves invisible, worthless, unimportant, not measuring up to others; feel empty most of the time; dread living and dread their life even when things are going well. Have difficulty receiving compliments and accolades. Will tear down what someone speaks about them. Have difficulty receiving love and affection. Wants it and longs for it but rejects it, cringes, and is guarded when it is given.

Spirit of the Victim - Causes spirits to enter a child's life through unresolved issues, pain, and wounds. Causes the child to constantly view themselves as a victim and to relive and rehearse hurts of the past. Child cannot receive love and happiness due to stuck in a victim mentality. The child will create situations where they are the victim. The child will sabotage victories so they can prove that life will always be full of pain, dread, and victimization. Drowns in sorrow and wants others to live there with them. Child views correction as punishment as if they are the victim rather than taking responsibility for actions and change life for the better.

Spirits of Deception & Trickery - Causes children to engage in lying, haughtiness, deceptive, manipulative, trickery behavior for self-gain, self-will, craftiness, cunningness. Behavior can range from petty to treacherous shrewdness. Causes the child to Infringe on the rights of others and violates the person's space, boundaries, morals, standards, virtue, with no regard to that person; will cause the child to discard or disregard the person after they have deceived, abused and used the person *(2Samuel 13).*

Spirits of Anti-Submissiveness & Disobedience - Cause children to defy and reject authority; they disregard rules, regulations, boundaries, and standards that authority figures out in place to keep them safe, lawful, honorable, honoring, and respecting the rights of others *(Proverbs 29:15, Proverbs 22:15, Mark 12:30, Colossians 3:20, Ephesians 6:1-3).*

Spirit of Absalom - Cause children to usurp and betray their parents, caregivers and/or authority figures. They will create and cause discontentment and strife between them and their parents, authority figures, etc. or between their parents and other people. They will gossip and spread lies and rumors, win the favor of others by exposing secrets, sins, and information, create scenarios to put them in favorable light while putting the parent, etc., in a negative light, set traps and snares to cause challenges for their parents, etc., gather others and information to strengthen their attack against their parents, etc., release an alternative vision that is more in favor of them than the parent or authority figure, set plans to literally kill their parents, caregivers, authority figures...*(2Samuel 15).*

Spirits of Death and Hell - Spirits sent to kill steal and destroy the life and destiny of a child. These spirits tend to follow the child from birth while releasing terror, tragedy, and/or hardship upon the child to stifle, delay, wound, afflict, murder the child's hope, and outlook on their life and future, and/or to literally take their lives so they will not fulfill their life's purpose

(Matthew 9:18, Matthew 9:23-25, Mark 5:22-24, Mark 5"38-43, Luke 8:41-55).

Spirits of Fear - Cause child to be fearful of the dark, going outside, being alone, going to sleep, attending school, engaging, building relationships, embarking upon life, trying new things, fear of engaging society. Spirits can grow up with children and cause them to become fearful panicky, anxious, stressful adults. Spirits will hide in children's rooms, under their beds, in their closets, in their mirrors, in and around their windows, and terrorize them at night. Uses the child to disrupt the peace and sleeping patterns of parents and family members in the home. Spirits of fear must be dealt with as can create an open door to mental illness, infirmities, and phobias *(Psalms 91, 2Timothy 1:7, 1John 4:18).*

Spirits of False Identity - These spirits create experiences, use experiences, hardships, word curses, generational curses, to release and confusion, distortion, misperceptions, brokenness, and breaks in a child's identity. These alterations cause parents and children to mold and shape children in an identity that is not the child's identity *(Deuteronomy 11:19, 2Timothy 3:5-7, 2Timothy 3:14-18, Psalms 8:2, Psalms 139, Isaiah 54:13 John 12:36).*

Spirits of Jezebel - Cause children to be controlling, manipulative, seductive, intimidating, overbearing, and overpowering towards, parents, siblings, family members, peers, teachers, etc. Such children are often prophets and leaders of God. This spirit likes to snatch them up early so that they become witches, warlocks, and prophets of the idol god Baal *(1Kings 16-22)*.

Spirits of Ahab - Cause children to be controlled by Jezebel parents, siblings, family members, peers, and peer groups. Children grow up passive, cowering, manipulated and slaves to Jezebel and bullies, fearing and dreading confrontation, having not voice, victims and with a victim mentality that often becomes rooted in their adult personality, while ruling their identity *(1Kings 16-22)*.

Spirits of Athaliah - This spirit identities and seeks to murder the royal seed - the chosen leaders in the family line. This spirit is ruthless towards grandchildren and extended seeds in the family line as it wants to rule in its stead. It is willing to stifle the blessings and growth of the family line by killing the seed so that it can reign. This spirit is vicious with words and released abusive actions to kill the hope, identity and life of its own grandchildren. Be careful leaving your children with bitter, no loving family members. Listen to your children when they state that they do not like spending the night or being around certain family members and when they are sharing words and actions that are demeaning, condemning and abusive in nature. Your child is probably revealing Athaliah who is murdering your child so that they can reign in their stead *(2Kings 11)*.

Spirits of Goliath - Bullying Spirits - This spirit mocks, belittles, brown eats, intimidated, cowers, physically and emotionally abuse children, shaping them to simulate Ahab, making them suicidal, making them living in the trenches of life in fear, rather than coming out and confronting life itself, wars, life challenges, and wanting to live and progress in life. These are your school and neighborhood bullies. They are vindictive and often unrepented. They get joy from beating and asserting power and fear over others. These children may have been taught this behavior by bullying parents or may be bound by a generational curse of Goliath. These children can appear friendly and helpful around authority figures then strike and attack in secret, in and among peers. This spirit will browbeat and abuse you the point when a child will feel suicide is the only option to being free from this spirit. It is important for parents to protect their children from Goliaths, expose and deal with children with these spirits, instill God identity in their child so they will know they have authority over Goliath *(Proverbs 22:10, 1Samuel 17)*.

Spirits of Jealous, Envy, & Comparison - Cause children to be jealous, resentful, begrudging, and covetous of others. Cause children to ridicule, stifle, reject, make light of, belittle and sabotage the advancement of others due to wanting to be them, being jealous of them, hating the favor that is on the child's life, hating that the child is better than them *(Genesis 4, Genesis 25:19-34, Genesis 37, 1Samuel 17)*.

Spirits that Mock - These spirits cause children to tease, taunt, laugh at, embarrass, acorn, ridicule, disrespect, terrorize, and poke fun at others to the point of cruelty, verbal abuse, and tormenting. *(2Kings 2:23-24)*.

Spirit of Saul - Causes a child to engage in behaviors of rivalry, competition, antagonism, ambition, strife, emulation, contention, pride, driving, striving, argument, pride, ego, strife, jealousy, envy, ambition. The child may even engage in vicious

110

and murderous acts to stifle, wound, afflict, or kill their competition so that they are the reigning competitor Even if the person is nice to the child, they are so driven by rivalry that they will have bouts of wanting to harm and prove they are better than the person *(1Samuel 18-19, James 4:1-2)*.

Spirit of the People Pleaser - Causes a child to seek to please others at the expense of their own identity, integrity and worship. Sacrifices their needs, desires, and value to be accepted and validated by others. Will even allow others to use them, abuse them, and take advantage of them so they can feel love, like they belong, and value *(Psalms 118:8, Ephesians 6:7)*.

Spirits of Worldliness - Cause a child to be carnal, fleshy, sinful, sensual, prideful, vain, materialistic, greedy; It causes a child to succumb to the spirit of the age rather than the will, plan and purpose of God. The child succumbs to mixture and/or the world's ways, while negating and defying the ways of God and his kingdom. These spirits will cause a child to use their gifts and callings for the world and for Satan for personal gain, wealth, and success. The focus is more on prosperity, awards, accolades, and personal advancement rather than glorifying God and advancing his kingdom. Many children get caught up in this system when their parents and caregivers are not submitted to God and are not seeking God for their destiny. Children result in living through the world systems and when they do come into understanding of God and their identity, they are having to be deprogrammed to fight their way out of the world's system, into God's system *(1Corinthians 2:12, Ephesians 2:1-3, Luke 11:15-32, 1John 2:16)*.

Spirits of Peer Pressure - Cause a child to yield to the pressures of peers, society, and culture in order to be valued, validated, fit in, or accepted. These pressures tend to draw a child into ungodliness, unholiness, and worldliness. They can also cause the child to be drawn away from God's identity and destiny for their lives *(Exodus 23:2, Proverbs 1:10, Daniel 3, Daniel 6, Romans 12:2, Ephesians 5:11).*

Spirits of Perversion - Causes a child to engage in twisted and perverted thinking and interactions; draws children into sexual curiosity before they are old enough to understand it and before they are grown and married. Sets up situations for children to succumb to the horrors of incest, molestation, rape, trafficking, masturbation, sodomy; homosexuality, lesbianism, pornography, uncleanness. These spirits can also cause children to experience gender confusion, sexual confusion, be attracted to the same sex, reject their gender and their sex. Preys on the purity, naivety and innocence of children by stealing and killing their virtue through perverse acts and experiences. Will also pervert children and use them to pervert other children *(1Samuel 2:12-36, 2Samuel 13), Matthew 17:17, Acts 2:40).*

Spirit of Lust - Cause a child to be drawn away from God through the lust of the eyes, lust of the flesh, and prides of life *(Numbers 11, Proverbs 6:25-26, Psalms 119:9-10, Ezekiel 23, Mark 7:20-23, 1John 2:16, 1Corinthians 1Thessalonians 3:4-5, 2Timothy 2:22, James 1:14-15).*

Spirits of Incubus and Succubus - These spirits prey on children through dreams and while they are asleep by entering their dreams and sleep realms and engaging them in perverted sexual acts. They will fondle children, masturbate them, rape them. These experiences awaken children's sexual appetite before the proper time and further draws them into sexual sin and secret sin when they ware awake *(Genesis 6:1-22, Jude 16-7, Ephesians 6:12).*

Spirits of Mare - The spirits cause children to have night terrors, nightmares, fear of going to sleep, fear of sleeping in their room, fear of the dark. These spirits attack in the dream realm or hide in children's rooms at night and instill fear in them. The child is scared and often in panic and terror due to the constant attacks from this spirit. It is important to listen to your children, pray over them, and their rooms in generally but especially when they have nightmares, speak of invisible playmates, or when they scared of the night and experiences occurring around there night and dream realms *(Job 4:13-16, Proverbs 3:24, Psalms 4:8, Psalms 91- terror by night).*

Spirits of Mental Illness - These spirits attack children's minds, emotions, and/or identity and cause severe and/or altered mental instability, split personalities, and extreme inability to cope in life, learn in life, advance in life. Spirits of mental illness can through a generational curse, attack when a child is in the womb, in the initial developmental stages of a child's life, when they start attending school, or in their preteen and teenage years. It is important to pray against generational curses in this area, govern your child's development, break word curses off their lives from authority figures and peers build them up in God identity'. It is important to be active in their school development and progression where you are engaging with teachers and even teaching teachers how to aide your child in learning, coping, and growing as they develop and learn and grow in destiny. Teach your children healthy coping, communication, conflict resolution, relational, and social skills so they can practice them daily and be helping in how they engage life and experiences *(Matthew 17:14-18, Mark 7:24-30, Mark 9:17-27)*.

Spirit of Insanity - Causes a child to have fits of being out of control, out of their mind, beside themselves. Child will display madness, confusion, impaired thinking, lunacy, mania, delirium, psychosis, derangement for no apparent reason or when they become stressed, threatened, upset, or challenged.

Spirit of Rage - Cause children to lend to fits of rage, anger, fury, retaliation, murderous words and actions, tantrums, wrath, passion, raving, blind rage, burning rage, and uncontrollable rage. These children may even physically and verbally abuse their parents, caregivers, authority figures, and peers during these episodes *(Proverbs 14:7, Proverbs 29:22, Ephesians 4:26, Ephesians 4:32, James 1:19-20)*.

Spirits of Restlessness & Anxiety - These spirits create situations and causes children to be stressed, apprehensive, tense, worry, dread, fear, be nervous, panic, be restlessness, uneasiness, fretful and inconsolable regarding life issues. These spirits can children to experience hyperactivity or attention deficit and even to be diagnosed with these disorders. Such labels open the door for children to be diagnosed with other mental disorders as other spirits come and bind and alter the personality and mental faculties of the child.

Death & Dumb Spirits - Cause children to be mute physically and spiritually where they may not be able to hear or speak. This spirit may also cloud a child's mind and mental faculties where they are unable to comprehend clearly, have trouble learning, have trouble communicating their needs, desires, thoughts, and feelings *(Mark 9:17-27, 2Timothy 3:7).*

Spirits of Cutting & Self-Harm - These spirits may cause children to bang their heads, cut themselves, pick at wounds that should be healing, create wounds then pick at them, deliberated hurt self for attention, bruise or break bones, pull their hair out, etc. These acts can be done to escape the pains of life, numb pain, release stress and anxiety, relieve feelings of hopelessness or helplessness, assert a sense of power over one's choices. These spirits and acts can sometimes be tied to witchcraft, idolatry, the spirit of Jezebel, and be a form of Baal worship. Jezebel and the idol god Baal require their worshippers to cut themselves and offer their blood as sacrifices to them. *(Deuteronomy 14:1-2, 1Kings 18:24, Leviticus 19:28, Psalms 34:18m Mark 5:2-5, 1Corinthians 6:12, 1Corinthians 6:19).*

Spirit of Arrested Development - These spirits cause trauma through some experience in childhood or finds a way to imprison the child's development in order to hinder them from growing into adulthood. The child's personality is not fully developed as parts of it is stuck at the age of trauma and/or arrested development. A spirit of the little girl and /or little may enter through this door and intertwine in the personality. They operate through a split identity where they are the arrested age one minute and their current age the next. The little girl and/or little boy spirit is literally seen in operation through them as they manifest tantrums, rage, passive aggressiveness, immaturity, foolishness, infantile, and juvenile delinquent behavior. The child will have delivered from trauma, the little girl/boy spirit will have to be cast out. Their personality will need to be prayed for so deliverance and healing can manifest and a commanding of the personality to grow up to their current age will have to be done where full mending and healing comes to the child's identity. If the little girl/boy spirit was intertwined in their personality, they will have to learn new healthy ways of behaving to fully mature in their personality and identity.

Attention Seeking Spirits - Cause children to do things to seek, demand, and command attention. Causes them to draw attention to themselves; thrives on any attention even negative attention as long as they are center stage. Will cause the child to be envious and compete with others for attention.

Spirit of Shyness - Rejection, self-consciousness, timidity, fear, hesitation, fear of rejection, withdrawal, apprehension, nervousness, bashfulness, low self-esteem.

Spirit of Low Self-Worth - Causes children to think in low and poor regard and self-image about themselves. Causes them to doubt their abilities, capabilities, value, and worth. Works with self-hatred and rejection of self and keeps the person for embodying their full worth.

Spirits of Infirmity - These spirits afflict, and infirm children with sickness, diseases, viruses, allergies, infections, to stifle their growth, development, and destiny. These attacks can come in the womb or while the child is growing up. Some children can battle long term affliction and infirmity by these spirits. Some children can even be bedridden or bound to the home, where they cannot go outside and play or at attend school. These spirits can attack through generational curses, sins of parents and others in the home, and because of a child's destiny and calling *(Psalms 34:19, Luke 9:38-43, Luke 7:11-15, John 4:46-52)*.

Spirit of Anorexia Nervosa - cause eating disorders in children. Causes them to starve themselves even unto severe sickness and death. Makes the child think they are fat, fear becoming fat; will provoke compulsive dieting and starvation to maintain desired weight. Usually hides in the eye gates as no matter how skinny the child is, they think they are fat and need to lose more weight. Child will self- reject, depressed, anxious, panicky; will isolate self to hide issues of starvation and obsession with weight.

Spirit of Bulimia Nervosa - Cause a child to binge eat and gorge lots of food then use methods to regurgitate or eliminate it from their bodies in order to lose weight and maintain weight. This spirit may work with spirits of lust, gluttony, pride, control. This spirit may be lodge in the eyes as the child is gripped with psychological warfare of body distortion; they have a poor image of their body battle thoughts and feelings of guilt or shame regarding eating, and their body image.

Consequences of Taking Prayer Out of School

Demon dealer, Madalyn Murray O'Hair was an American activist supporting atheism and separation of church and state. The demon dealing atheist campaigned against the church's influence publicly and politically. A demon dealer is a person who presents an alternative way of existing and living that negates and draws people away from God and his identity and purpose for their lives. Their theories sound reasonable and as if it benefits all mankind, yet it has no biblical foundation or truth, and ultimately drives people to denounce and sin against God.

Long before the likes of Stephen Hawking, another demon dealing atheist who lobbied the theories of creationism and intellectual design, which are belief systems that attempt to debunk the existence of God, O'Hair gained notoriety for helping to push Bible readings and prayer out of schools. O'Hair sued the Baltimore Public School System for requiring her son to read the Bible as a school activity. Her case went all the way to the Supreme Court and ended prayer in public schools in 1963. Prayer is still banned to this day.

In 1963 O'Hair founded American Atheists and served as its president until 1986, after which her son Jon Garth Murray succeeded her. She created the first issues of American Atheist Magazine. The American Atheists Foundation is still in operation today. They relentlessly lobby to establish anti-religious laws and agendas, and campaign against political leaders who desire to keep the true and living God - Jesus Christ - as the only God of our nation. The American Atheist also war to restrict the right to acknowledge and serve Jesus Christ and to implement his Biblical principles and an uncompromised gospel into religious institutions, charitable organizations, businesses, and societal arenas. O'Hair devoted her life to contending against and dismantling the powers of the church. She was known as the most hated woman in the world and gloated in this title as she released her demon dealing agenda of hatred against God in the earth.

We as believers have taken lightly the power that prayer and Bible studies being taken out of schools have had on our children, our destinies, and our society. I want to share a few pointers of how it has impacted our children so we cannot just SHIFT to reverse laws that restrict religious practices in school settings, but prick us as believers to build our own schools where educational curriculum and trades include the worshipping and learning of God, journeying with God in covenant relationship, Bible study, building of godly character, living through biblical standards, and training and equipping of destiny.

The following are the result of prayer removed from school:

God is no longer the foundation of a child's gifts, talents, and education. There foundation is full of mixture and is not solid in the identity, blueprint, and standards of God.

Children spend six to eight hours a day without communicating with God their creator. They are receiving from a system that is full of manmade and demonic ideologies and practices.

Blank mind meditation, yoga, tapping, and other demonic, manmade, or frivolous new age practices are being used to calm children and assist them with coping with life stressors rather than relying on the power of the Holy Spirit to deliver, heal, teach, and guide them in releasing anxiety and tackling day to day experiences.

Children are taught and trained in destiny outside the presence and voice of God. Parents have to trust teachers and authority to train and equip their children in destiny, while hoping they are releasing the voice, will, and plan of God unto children's lives.

Children are not taught how to combat demonic oppression, possession, and demonic peer pressure. They are made to live among, accept, and include these forces and beliefs into their lives; and to succumb to behavior and cultural modification regarding how to accommodate these forces and beliefs into their lives.

Children are penalized, teased, and punished for praying, reading the Bible, and utilizing godly principles to deal with demonic and unhealthy teachers, peers, worldly rules, laws, beliefs and systems, social and cultural standards.

Children are pressured to conform to the worldly educational systems' laws and belief system, and to comprise the word and gospel of Jesus Christ.

Mixture of serving the devil and the world and worshiping and considering idol gods is taught and instilled in children. They are provided false truths concerning alternative ways to salvation and eternal life, and with covenant of destiny with imposter gods that are not their true creator - Jesus Christ - the true and loving God.

Fame, fortune, success, and approval of man, becomes the focus and drive for destiny, rather than seeking God for his design purpose and blueprint for who and how a child is to impact and influence the earth; and to do the will of that which pleases God and give him glory.

Children are taught and made to display morals and values that are good thoughts and beliefs but can include manmade and demon acceptance and regard for matters that are not pleasing to God.

Children are not rooted in the love and ability to esteem others higher than when selves, so self-absorbed prideful living agendas override their personality, behavior, and approach to success and life itself.

God is SHIFTED out of community and societal living and out of homes and generational lines. Children grow up and live life void of a sufficient foundation of God rooted in their identity, actions, relationships, gifts and talents.

Often our ministers are preaching within the sectors of the body of Christ or evangelizing the lost in communities. Rarely have we had a minister who impacted laws the ways the demon dealing O'Hair done, such that it gives a voice to God and his people. Many Old Testament leaders, and New Testament disciples and apostles opposed injustices, unrighteousness decrees, and worldly and idolatrous governmental systems, as they waged religious war against Tribes, kingdoms, governments. As we study the Bible, we can find them being established in governments to enact the will of God in the land or preaching and teaching in the synagogues and contended against the injustices that defied God and enslaved the people. I decree that a SHIFT will occur where marketplace ministers will take their place in political and business arenas and contend to successfully establish God's laws and practices.

❖ Our children need you to be a voice for them.
❖ The body of Jesus Christ need you to be a voice for them.
❖ Jesus Christ needs you to be in voice, his representative, his law, and kingdom in the earth.

Lord even now we ask you to give parents and spiritual leaders keen eye sight to identify the children and believers who are law makers and law changers; also provide them with strategic wisdom and strategy of how to train, equip, release, and cover them as the operate in their calling.

We call then forth!
We launch them forth!
We SHIFT them forth!

For such a time as this! SHIFT!

Spiritual Law Contenders In The Bible

Shadrach, Meshach, and Abednego were thrown into the fiery furnace by Nebuchadnezzar, king of Babylon, when they refuse to bow down to the king's image. A fourth image, Jesus Christ, joined them in the fire, saving them from harm. The king sees the fourth man walking in the flames. He establishes a decree that any people, nation, or language which speaks anything amiss against the God of Shadrach, Meshach, and Abednego shall be cut in pieces, and their houses shall be made an ash heap; because there is no other God who can deliver like this (*Daniel 3*).

Joseph and Daniel were upstanding young men who served in civil government, exerting influence to further the flourishing of their nations (*Genesis 37-50, Daniel 6*).

Matthew the tax collector, worked for the government of Roman and eventually became a disciple of Jesus Christ. (*Matthew 9:9-13, Mark 2:13-17, Luke 5:27-32*)

Jesus was born with the ultimate government, the kingdom of heaven, upon his shoulders.

Isaiah 9:6-7 For unto us a child is born, unto us a son is given: and the government shall be upon his shoulder: and his name shall be called Wonderful, Counsellor, The mighty God, The everlasting Father, The Prince of Peace. Of the increase of his government and peace there shall be no end, upon the throne of David, and upon his kingdom, to order it, and to establish it with judgment and with justice from henceforth even forever. The zeal of the Lord of hosts will perform this.

Jesus was killed by the government of Roman due to religious leaders seeing him as a threat for preaching the gospel (Study the gospels).

Paul's life can be studied as he had several run ins with the government of his day. Paul and Silas thrown in jail for casting the devil out of the fortune telling diviner of the Delphi government (**Study Acts 16**).

The contenders lived in the world infiltrating political and worldly systems but did not succumb to them. Our leaders of our day must be able to do the same as the scriptures mandate us to have clear distinct boundaries about who our God is and what kingdom we serve.

John 15:19 *If ye were of the world, the world would love his own: but because ye are not of the world, but I have chosen you out of the world, therefore the world hateth you.*

John 18:36 *Jesus answered, My kingdom is not of this world: if my kingdom were of this world, then would my servants fight, that I should not be delivered to the Jews: but now is my kingdom not from hence.*

Romans 12:2 *And be not conformed to this world: but be ye transformed by the renewing of your mind, that ye may prove what [is] that good, and acceptable, and perfect, will of God.*

1John 2:15 Love not the world, neither the things [that are] in the world. If any man love the world, the love of the Father is not in him.
John 17:14 I have given them thy word; and the world hath hated them, because they are not of the world, even as I am not of the world.

John 8:23 And he said unto them, Ye are from beneath; I am from above: ye are of this world; I am not of this world.

Ephesians 6:12 For we wrestle not against flesh and blood, but against principalities, against powers, against the rulers of the darkness of this world, against spiritual wickedness in high [places].

Colossians 3:2 Set your affection on things above, not on things on the earth.

When those in the Bible opposed worldly governments or even worked for them, they did not succumb to the world or their standards. There work was also not for the world's system but for God's. This is what he needs as we train and equip our children and believers to infiltrate political and governmental realms and spheres. We need them to stand, speak, and make sure the law honor and protect God's kingdom, standards, and his people.

In 2020, President Donald Trump updated the religious freedom act to safeguard individuals who desire to engage in religious principles and practices to do so without being protested.

Freedom of religion is a principle that supports the freedom of an individual or community, in public or private, to manifest religion or belief in teaching, practice, worship, and observance. It also includes the freedom to change one's religion or beliefs.

Though this did not include mandatory prayer or studying of the word as a school curriculum, it does protect the teachers and students who desire to do so during school hours. Moreover, it protects churches, ministries, businesses, and organizations from being sued due to the desire to follow biblical principles. This is important because during the presidency of Barrack Obama, laws were enacted, dethroning religious liberty as a central pillar in America's political and civil life. Laws were instituted requiring those of religious sectors to serve all people despite their religious biblical beliefs and restricted those in religious sectors from exercising their biblical standards and religious rights should someone of the opposite belief system desire a service from them. Many religious believers were sued, and some lost their ministries and businesses due to being sued for standing in and operating through biblical standards. President Trump restored these rights to religious believers. However, we see from these two presidencies that the religious freedom can be legislated by the worldly government and can change depending who is in office. We need godly leaders in position to assert our right to serve God and live through his biblical standards. We need such leaders identified and cultivated from the womb, and we need parents advocating for laws that protect our rights in this area.

I decree a SHIFT is taking place right now to raise such leaders from the womb. I call the righteous justice leaders and prophets from birth. May they be born with obvious godly indignation for God's word, purposes, and plans. May their parents identify them, protect them, train and equip them for who God will require them to be as his righteous judges in the earth. **SHIFT RIGHT NOW! SHIFT!**

A Soul-Wounded Parent

When a parent is carrying soul wounds, their parenting style often includes the following:

Feel entitled to give your children everything they want or the things you wished for as a child, while teaching them no value for working for what they want or honoring your hard work in purchasing things for them.

Pamper the child unnecessarily. Lacking balance in who you view and engage the child; demanding others do the same regardless of the child's behavior.

Overly protective of the child. Restrict the child of liberties due to constant unrealistic or anxious fears that something may happen to the child.

Are too lenient in your liberty with the child. There is a lack of enough protection where the child is exposed to dangers, activities, situations, topics, that are not age appropriate or risk their safety.

Want to be viewed as the cool parent. Do not govern what they watch, listen to, participate in, where they go, who they are with.

Fear setting proper rules, boundaries, punishments, and consequences with your children for fear of hurting their feelings, fear they will be mad at you, or believing they will feel unloved.

Overly disciplining and punishing your children due to your own unresolved childhood issues. For example, being severely punished or abused as a child; fearing your child will turn out to be a horrible adult or fear of them being like you, your mate, or others family members.

Lack balance with sharing the parenting role. Want your spouse to do all the disciplining while you look like the good parent; you get your need for love, approval, and acceptance met by positioning yourself as the good parent and letting your spouse be viewed as the uncaring horrible disciplinarian.

Remind them constantly that they are like "so and so,". You punish and verbally abuse them for looking like the person, acting like the person, remind you of that person. They grow up under the bondage of this false perpetuated identity that is really your soul wound pain being bestowed upon them, rather than being cultivated in their true pure identity.

Compare your children one to another and pit them against one another. Spark sibling rivalry.

Always giving advice, lecturing, criticizing, belittling or ridiculing, but no or minimal esteeming or empowerment.

May not or do not possess the ability to encourage, reward or accolade your child.

Fail to support the child in their pursuits and successes.

Do not spend time with the child. Always busy working or doing things that take away from parenting, loving, supporting, training, equipping, and empowering the child. Make excuses for your actions; reprimand the child for wanting time or for misbehaving to gain your attention or time rather than changing and making time for the child.

Compete with your child for attention, position, rewards, accolades. You strip your child of honor when they achieve heights and even take credit for their accomplishments.

Do not regard your child's feelings; you say whatever you want to say to them - however you want to say it - with not regard for how it impacts them.

Strip the child of having a voice by demanding them to be silent only, while refusing to hear their thoughts, or allowing them to share their thoughts or feelings. Make them express their thoughts and feelings based on gender roles where boys "man up" and girls are "drama queens" rather than teaching them balanced and healthy communication, conflict resolution, coping, and relationship skills. Punishing them when they express their thoughts and feelings or assert their right to have a voice, especially when they are right in their perspective.

Have your child serving in roles that a spouse, mother, father, friend, mentor, leader, should be playing in your life. They are filling voids and needs that other adults should be fulfilling for you.

Lack the responsibility to sufficiently provide or to be a parent so your child is the parent. They may be cooking, cleaning, working to pay bills or provide for the needs of the family, taking care of their siblings, running errands and engaging in activities to keep the home afloat.

Engage in behavior that negatively impacts the child, the household, and their perspective of family. For example: sexual, physical, verbal, spiritual, abuse; neglect, mental instability, excessive drinking, partying, doing drugs, prostitution, whoredom, having different people and lovers in the home, adultery; constantly leaving kids with family members, friends, acquaintances, lovers, strangers.

You are a poor example such that your child mimics your behavior and poor choices.

Do not provide a solid godly spiritual foundation of family and God for the child because of what you experienced or did not experience in these areas as a child. Leaving it up to the child to decide if they want to go to church, attend ministry events, pray, study their Bible; decide whether they want to serve the true and living God, an idol, or if they want to be atheist. Allowing the child to engage in witchcraft practices and mixture.

These soul wound parenting styles hinder the identity and destiny of children. It also distorts their perception of God and his biblical principles and standards for life, family, and destiny fulfillment. It is important to be delivered and healed of soul issues that would hinder you from parenting effectively and sufficiently. Until you are healed, you cannot parent through a pure well that governs your household and your child's destiny.

Genesis 18:19 *For I know him, that he will command his children and his household after him, and they shall keep the way of the LORD, to do justice and judgment; that the LORD may bring upon Abraham that which he hath spoken of him.*

Deuteronomy 4:9 New King James Bible *Only take heed to yourself, and diligently keep yourself, lest you forget the things your eyes have seen, and lest they depart from your heart all the days of your life. And teach them to your children and your grandchildren.*

Ephesians 6:4 *And, ye fathers, provoke not your children to wrath: but bring them up in the nurture and admonition of the Lord.*

The Amplified Bible *Fathers, do not irritate and provoke your children to anger [do not exasperate them to resentment], but rear them [tenderly] in the training and discipline and the counsel and admonition of the Lord.*

SHIFT! SHIFT RIGHT NOW!

Stewardship! Me? A Mother? Why?
Minister Brandie Reese's Testimony

I remember receiving so many prophetic words about the children I would have once married. I would laugh it off because I thought *"this is just what people say to newlyweds."* I never saw myself being someone's mother. Even though part of my nature is motherly, I never thought about being a mother.

I remember the day I found out I was pregnant; I was a nervous wreck. I had no expectations. Despite being married and in a godly covenant, I was afraid. I began thinking about all the things that were going on in my life at that time. I thought *"how could I be pregnant at a time like this?"* I thought about everything I would have to sacrifice. I had no idea what being a mother looked like, but none of this matter to God. He started giving me dreams during my pregnancy about the baby I was carrying and His plan for her. This is where the Lord would require something of me, that he requires from every parent. He was SHIFTING me into understanding that responsibility leads to obedience and stewardship.

STEWARDSHIP:

What does God think about stewardship in general and what does he think about it in regard to parenting.

From Genesis to Revelation, you will find a common theme of stewardship.

Adam and Eve had to steward over the garden. They had to steward the presence of God in the Garden.

Moses and Aaron had to steward over the people of Israel.

All of the Kings (righteous and evil), had to steward over their kingdoms

Mary had to steward over Jesus.

The Apostle Paul had to steward the teachings of Jesus. Apostle Paul was also a spiritual father to Timothy, so he had to steward over that relationship.

Stewardship entails administering, employee int, attending to, and managing something on someone else's behalf. In this case we are talking about managing the destiny of the God has given us. MY LORD!

Since children are given to us as a blessing from the Lord, it requires his plans, his wisdom, his wants, his desires, his word, to be implemented in our stewardship over them. It takes a personal relationship with him to steward properly and with divine vision. For Psalms 127:3 declares that children are a reward from the Lord, but they MUST be stewarded over, from conception and when they are birthed into this challenging world.

When God births forth, he starts in seed form, and as the seed grows, it matures into full identity. One of the greatest seed forms we have is Jesus and the gospel that was birthed through him.

Matthew 2:13 The Message Bible This is how Jesus the Messiah was born. His mother, Mary, was engaged to be married to Joseph. But before the marriage took place, while she was still a virgin, she became pregnant through the power of the Holy Spirit.

Though fully God, Jesus humbled himself and started in seed form through the power of the Holy Spirit.

John 1:14 And the Word was made flesh, and dwelt among us, (and we beheld his glory, the glory as of the only begotten of the Father,) full of grace and truth.

Philippians 2:5-8 Let this mind be in you, which was also in Christ Jesus: Who, being in the form of God, thought it not robbery to be equal with God: But made himself of no reputation, and took upon him the form of a servant, and was made in the likeness of men: And being found in fashion as a man, he humbled himself, and became obedient unto death, even the death of the cross.

Jesus was given a destiny to save the world and Mary had to steward over his life and destiny.

Luke 1:30-36 And the angel said unto her, Fear not, Mary: for thou hast found favour with God. And, behold, thou shalt conceive in thy womb, and bring forth a son, and shalt call his name JESUS. He shall be great, and shall be called the Son of the

Highest: and the Lord God shall give unto him the throne of his father David: And he shall reign over the house of Jacob for ever; and of his kingdom there shall be no end. Then said Mary unto the angel, How shall this be, seeing I know not a man? And the angel answered and said unto her, The Holy Ghost shall come upon thee, and the power of the Highest shall overshadow thee: therefore also that holy thing which shall be born of thee shall be called the Son of God.

Mary did not conceive Jesus; therefore, she was put in charge to steward over him. She was given the seed of salvation and told to birth it, nurture it, cultivate it, train it, equip it, and release it into destiny. Despite the reproach that would have come upon her for being pregnant without being married first, she knew she was birthing someone special from heaven, and was honored to attend to the seed of the Lord.

This should be the case for all mothers. We should be willing to tend to – steward – the power seed that God puts in our wound.

As we read **Verse 46–55**, we find Mary singing a prophetic song,

- ✓ Glorifying God
- ✓ Rejoicing in who God was
- ✓ Expressing humility for being chosen to steward Jesus
- ✓ Decreeing generational inheritance
- ✓ Decreeing how Jesus' destiny will fulfill ancestor all promises and prophecies
- ✓ Decreeing the impact Jesus will have generations
- ✓ Decreeing the goodness, mercy, and prosperity of who he is – his identity

✓ Decreeing the salvation of who Jesus is
✓ Decreeing the eternity of who Jesus is as his destiny saves the world

My soul doth magnify the Lord, And my spirit hath rejoiced in God my Saviour. For he hath regarded the low estate of his handmaiden: for, behold, from henceforth all generations shall call me blessed. For he that is mighty hath done to me great things; and holy is his name. And his mercy is on them that fear him from generation to generation. He hath shewed strength with his arm; he hath scattered the proud in the imagination of their hearts. He hath put down the mighty from their seats, and exalted them of low degree. He hath filled the hungry with good things; and the rich he hath sent empty away. He hath holpen his servant Israel, in remembrance of his mercy; As he spake to our fathers, to Abraham, and to his seed for ever.

This prophetic song was breathing the identity and purpose of God into Mary's womb and upon the seed – Jesus. It was in accordance to what the Angel had told her about Jesus. She also had the right posture about being pregnant. Both are key principles to stewarding the destiny of children from the womb. In that regard, I want to ask,

➢ *What are you speaking over your baby?*
➢ *What are you consuming both naturally and spiritually that can and will have an impact on your baby?*

Even from the womb, babies are aware of the world outside the womb. They can hear and sense what is going on around them.

A study conducted by Professor Stanislas Dehaene, who studies experimental cognitive brain psychology, states that *"The cortex, which is the epicenter of human consciousness, starts to form by six months gestation. Even Neuroscientists suspect from studies that even within the womb, in the late stages of pregnancy, the baby becomes familiar with the sound of its mother's voice and may already be learning language."* The study also states that *"While it's impressive that a fetus responds to the sounds of its mother's voice when in the womb, Dehaene points out that the brain can process language without consciousness."*

In another study conducted by science-direct, they had pregnant women agree to saying a specific passage everyday consistently for the last 6 weeks of their pregnancy. Once the babies were born, they conducted a operant - choice procedure test to determine whether the sounds or words of the daily passage spoken from their mother had more of an effect on them than just random sayings, and it was determined that the daily passage spoken by the mother had more of an re-enforcement (effect) than just random sayings.

It goes without saying that both studies prove that Proverbs 18:21 is true, *"Life and death are in the power of the tongue."* When Elizabeth, John the Baptist's mother, received a visit from Mary, the baby leaped inside of Elizabeth. Her baby leaped after hearing Mary's voice. Both baby AND mother were filled with the Holy Ghost.

Luke 1:41-44 And it came to pass, that, when Elisabeth heard the salutation of Mary, the babe leaped in her womb; and

Elisabeth was filled with the Holy Ghost: And she spake out with a loud voice, and said, Blessed art thou among women, and blessed is the fruit of thy womb. And whence is this to me, that the mother of my Lord should come to me? For, lo, as soon as the voice of thy salutation sounded in mine ears, the babe leaped in my womb for joy.

Do you see how powerful that is? What the mother received, the baby did also, and responded! Think about that.

It is very important for mothers to be aware of what they are saying, what they are doing, who they are allowing to speak into their lives and the lives of their babies. YES, even while pregnant.

As I mentioned earlier, when I was pregnant, God would give me dreams concerning my children. I would wake up from my dreams, pray into what I saw, and make declarations over their lives in agreement with what the God showed me.

> ➢ *What is God showing you?*
> ➢ *What is he telling you?*
> ➢ *What is he instructing you to do daily while pregnant?*
> ➢ *What is he requiring of you regarding the children you have now?*
> ➢ *What does he want you to implement to cultivated their lives and destiny?*

Let's discuss the reason it is important to have God's biblical perspective of children and family:

During a very challenging day with my children, I finally asked God, *"What was it...What in your mind that made you think that I was fit to be a mother...Why did you make me a mother?"* I expressed to God that parenting was hard and frustrating and quite frankly something I never asked to have.

You see, I was not one of those young girls who dreamed of getting married or having children. When I would journal, I never prayed or asked God for children or a husband. My plans were to be a career woman and live my best life doing me. However, somehow, I ended up in God's plan and I dreaded it. My Lord. *"Here I am, why God?"* *"Why would you interrupt my plans?"*

God responded, *"Why don't you just ask me the real question?"*

Me: *"What real question...That IS my real question....Why did you give me children?"*

God: *"No daughter, what you're really asking me is why did I give you RESPONSIBILITY. You know the one thing most people don't want from me. You asked me to show you my ways, the way of the kingdom, the way of my heart...Family is the way to my heart. Family is My idea. Not yours. I am rewriting history in your bloodline, and you don't even see it."*

Me: Silence....

As I listened to God, I recognized that my plans were void of true responsibility, servanthood, and stewardship. In fact, my plans regarding marriage and children were extremely selfish

140

and self-satisfying. It was not until I started journeying into motherhood, (which is a form of servanthood in the eyes of God), that I realized I was selfish, and did not want to submit my life to a greater work and calling.

Motherhood and parenting are and will forever be God's idea. It requires submission, servanthood, and stewardship. The design of family is meant to reflect the kingdom, and how God is revealed to us and those in the world. It was never God's intention for us to do life alone. Family is huge to God. In fact, family is his way to cast away loneliness.

We see this throughout scripture. In *Genesis*, when God realized that Adam was alone, He stated, *"It is NOT good for man to be alone."* He was not just talking about Adam, but it was a reference to the human nature. Therefore, God created a woman, Eve, and the two of them immediately became family. As they joined together, God established them as family. God then placed them in the garden of Eden and gave them stewardship over their covenant marriage, the animals, the earth, who they were as they built family.

Genesis 1:26-28 *And God said, Let us make man in our image, after our likeness: and let them have dominion over the fish of the sea, and over the fowl of the air, and over the cattle, and over all the earth, and over every creeping thing that creepeth upon the earth. So God created man in his own image, in the image of God created he him; male and female created he them. And God blessed them, and God said unto them, Be fruitful, and multiply, and replenish the earth, and subdue it: and have*

dominion over the fish of the sea, and over the fowl of the air,
and over every living thing that moveth upon the earth.

Adam and Eve was responsible for the stewardship over their family and multiply mankind in the earth. **Psalms 68:6** contends, *"God setteth solitary in a family."* The **New Living Bible** states, *"God places the lonely in family."* This means God establishes unity, togetherness, love, covenant, fulfillment.

Society has made motherhood to be this inconvenient, not right now, how can this be happening, burden, how do I get rid of it, JOB. All of these thoughts reflect a worldly perspective of children and motherhood. Nowhere in scripture does God make any such references regarding motherhood. In fact, he says the opposite. Motherhood is an honor. It is a responsibility. It is stewardship. It is sacred and should be revered as such.

As mothers, it is our responsibility to nurture our children, love them, teach them, grow them up in the word, teach them the ways of Jesus, teach them about family, teach them responsibility, and give them a rich heritage and legacy of Love. This is important because children are image bearers. They are like you, created in the image of God, and reflect the nature of God. What we pour into them will be replicated when they grow up. Cultivating Jesus in them, enables them to replicate him – his God image that was instilled in them at birth. Why not allow them to have the biblical perspective of themselves and God?

There are many myths concerning motherhood that are not biblical. Below are three of most common myths. Please keep in mind when reading scripture, it is important to know the right context, content, era, and audience-none of the scriptures were written from a twenty first century lens.

Pregnancy and birth are a curse because of Eve's disobedience.

This is far from the truth and is not Biblical at all. Think about it? Why would God curse what he created? I love the way biblical teacher Phylicia Masonheimer corrects this erroneous thinking biblically. She writes, *"God only cursed the ground and the serpent. He did not curse women. Humanity's sin, though initiated by Eve came through Adam (Romans 5), left the world resistant and flawed. Man and woman would labor (same word) to bring forth life from the ground and body. Woman was not especially cursed. Birth is not a terrible destiny. Rather the Bible speaks of the glory of being a woman."*

Children are a BURDEN.

False! The word declares that children are a REWARD and an INHERITANCE from God.

Psalms 127:3 New Living Bible *Children are a gift from the Lord; they are a reward from him."*

Your life is over because you are a mother.

Society would have you to believe that your baby is a *"thief"* because they are *"stealing"* your life.

False! The word declares that Jesus came to give you LIFE, and that more abundantly. With Long life, will HE satisfy you! What a promise!

John 10:10 American Standard Bible The thief cometh not, but that he may steal, and kill, and destroy: I came that they may have life, and may have it abundantly."

Psalms 91:15 American Standard Bible With long life will I satisfy him, And show him my salvation.

To summarize, being a mother is a gift from God! It is a Holy call. It is joyous. It is beautiful. God always desired it to be joyous! Because we as mothers are a blessing to God. We serve our families as unto him.

Psalms 113:9 American Standard Bible He maketh the barren woman to keep house, And to be a joyful mother of children.

Stewarding God's Way
Minister Brandie Reese's Charge

Stewardship over what is put in the body:

The scriptures declare that our bodies are a temple of the Holy Ghost. This is the same for children, even babies. We must steward over what they consume. This includes, food, beverages, medicines, herbs, medications, preventative medicines and vaccinations, medical procedures and practices.

There are organizations and companies that create products that are specifically targeting children, and yes, these products cause harm.

One of the greatest attacks against children right now aside from child sexual trafficking, abortion, and abuse, is the push for vaccines. Are you aware that when a baby is born, one of the main aims of doctors is to vaccinate your children, and if you have boys, they promote circumcision.

There are very harmful ingredients in vaccines that will and do cause harm. One of the main harmful ingredients is *Polysorbate 80*, which is a preservative. When this chemical is injected, it opens up the blood brain barrier, and allows for other harmful chemicals to come in and they collectively began altering the brain. Vaccines have never been tested for safety, especially on pregnant women or those who have immunocompromised. Parents would have to do research and seek God regarding the truth concerning vaccinations and how it impacts children, especially how it would impact their children. It is important to research the testimonies of the mothers who children have been negatively affected by vaccinations. These have sounded the alarm regarding how vaccines have either injured their children or caused death. Many nurses and doctors are also speaking candidly on the harmful effects of vaccinations. The substances in vaccinations are shared as if they are harmless, but they are DNA and life altering impacts that can rarely be reversed once they enter the blood and body system of your child.

There is an entire website about vaccine injury from thousands of parents who have lost their children from vaccines. When a vaccine is administered by a doctor, and there is ANY type of reaction, the hospital or medical staff is supposed to report the injury to a system called VAERS (please research VAERS). Many of these reactions go unreported. This is because there is big money in vaccinations. The hospital and medical staff receive financial restitution for every child they vaccinate. They will lose this easy, profitable side hustle, if vaccines are viewed as harmful.

Vaccines are one of the main reasons immune systems become compromised. Did you know that aborted fetus tissue is in the flu shot and in other vaccines? Did you know that vaccines are LIVE once they are administered to the body, and can live on the skin for up to twenty days? If a person gets the flu shot, they are carrying the live virus with and on them for twenty-one days? This means the person can spread a strand of the flu. This is the reason children become sick at the beginning of the school year when vaccines are administered. They are carrying and spreading vaccine sicknesses in and from their bodies. This is possibly some of the reason for mental illnesses such as increase of autism, attention deficit disorder, hyperactivity, and could be a reason many children are having gender altering issues. If live dead fetus tissue is being injected into their bodies, this DNA is mixing into and interfering with their genetic makeup. Such interruptions is causing a confusion as the child's personality, identity, body structure, and body systems, seeks to navigate the changes that are occurring inside of them. Our DNA was never meant to be mixed or altered. Nothing foreign or of another human being, should be placed in our bodies and seen as good. This is DEMON DEALING in its rawest form.

Did you know that on the real vaccine insert and packaging, which is about two foot long, not the little information packets they hand out at the doctor's office, tells individuals that after being vaccinated to stay away from infants, children, and the elderly? Did you know that pediatricians GAIN a monetary reward for vaccinating your babies? I had to throw that in their again, as this is a money game and we the pawns sacrificing our children so that demon dealers can become rich off our ignorance and lack of stewardship in this area.

Did you know......well, you would HAVE to do research to learn more. That is my stewardship challenge to you. Study vaccines and ask God to reveal to you the truth about their purpose regarding children and our lives in general.

Stewardship over their eyes:

Are you aware that social media on all platforms, movies, TV shows, etc., are wanting to indoctrinate your children to give them nonbiblical perspectives? It is your job as parents to govern what your children watch and see. GET TO STEWARDING RIGHT NOW IN JESUS NAME! SHIFT! *Stewardship over their ears:*

- ✓ *What and who are you allowing your to listen to?*
- ✓ *Who are you allowing to speak to them, and into them?*
- ✓ *What music are they listening to? What shows are they watching?*

You MUST set and keep godly standards.

- ✓ *What is God saying?*
- ✓ *What has he told you concerning your children? MAY AN URGENCY HIT YOU TO ASK HIM RIGHT NOW!*
- ✓ *Are you fearful of what people will say or think because of the standards?*
- ✓ *Will you follow man or will you follow God?*

I thank God for the revelation that Taquetta and Shannon have and what they has poured out in this book. This book offers insight into how to biblically govern over your children.

When I met Taquetta, I was not a mother or a wife yet. She came along and journeyed (still is) with me and taught me the true things of God. She would teach me how to discern movies, music, tv shows, etc. I am forever thankful for her life!!! She has helped me have grace for those who think I do too much in governing my children. I understand that I am a curse breaker and that the only way the kingdom blessings of God can flow to my children and their children and on and on, is through my stewardship of their souls and destinies. I can stand in the face of adversity from family members, friends, acquaintances, teachers, believers, who want to compromise the gospel or who want me to compromise what God has spoken regarding my children and their destiny. I know that certain disobedience on my part can mean the death of them. I reject spiritual and natural death upon their lives by being obedient to God at the expense of having favor with man.

The principals that Taquetta and Shannon share in this book are worth exploring and investing in. One of the greatest gifts Taquetta has ever given me was teaching me how to go to God for myself. She taught me how to hear from God and how to live a joyous and fulfilled life in him. She saw in me, what I did not yet see in myself, and journeys with me from a future me standpoint and a generation standpoint regarding my children and lineage. She constantly reminds me of who I am in God and how he sees me, my husband, and my seed.

I remember having conversations with her, which at the time was scary, about being a wife and mother. She would process with me and pray in covenant with me. She would give me small doses of wisdom at a time, and she would teach me how to process, evolve, and go back to God and evolve again! My whole point to you is to DO WHAT GOD SAID! Use this book as a tool to STEWARD your seed and let God bless their destiny. **SHIFT RIGHT NOW! SHIFT!**

Teaching Children a Daily Walk with the Lord

Learn each of your children's personalities; learn to enjoy their identities, what they bring to your life, and who they are in the earth.

Train, equip and engage your children according to their divine blueprint.

Have a daily relationship with your child. Not just in hard times, good destiny moments, when they are good, or when they are bad. Be conscious to do life with them and to teach and empower them every day.

Pray over and with your children at night, in the morning before they go off the school, and when they return.

Pray with them before meals and have them pray.

Set times to pray, worship, praise, and study the Bible with your child. Teach your children how to pray and teach them how to love God with all their heart, all their mind, all their soul.

Teach your children who God is, who they are praying too, and the importance of praying.

Teach your children how to identify the voice and presence of the Lord.

Teach your children relationship before you engage them in religious church and ministry practices.

Work with your children to be filled with the Holy Spirit. Teach them the purpose of the Holy Spirit, to use their prayer language, and how to commune and grow in the authority, character, fruit, and gifts of the Holy Spirit. Teach them godly morals and values and how to SHIFT more into them as they grow with the Holy Spirit.

Teach your child how to pray and seek God for answers and direction, especially during challenging times, role model this to them so their faith can be built to trust God as their source.

Get some music cd's, children's books, coloring book, games, that teach your children about God and connect them to God. Do not use the lack of a resources to dictate what you can provide your child. Make your own and tailor it to the way your child learns, their identity and their destiny.

Study the children and teenage characters from the Bible with your children so they will know that it is biblical to serve God at a young age.

Teach your children how to contend for the faith - how to stand in the word, promises and prophecies of God. Teach them the importance of not compromising and how not to compromise.

Teach your child to love purity, holiness, righteousness and virtue. Teach them how important thee characteristics are to their calling. Teach them the destiny standards they need to sustain in these characteristics.

Keep entertainment pure and repent and adjust quickly when it is not pure so your child would know how to govern their purity. Consistently pray over your home and let your child witness this, teach your child to pray over their room and to keep their atmosphere filled with God.

Cultivate your home and child's room with godly music and scriptures, especially as they sleep to close their dream realm.

Emphasize obedience and teach your child how this is important to God, their covenant with him, their destiny and calling. Give them room to make mistakes and to grow, while also teaching them that God is perfecting them as they are obedient to him.

Live what you instill in your children so they will not be desensitized to the things of God.

Live who you are in ministry, at church, and in public, who you are in private so your child will not compromise regarding the things of God.

You learn to love God and his purpose for your life so you can role model this to your child.

Ask your children about their day and use these moments to draw them into God, obedience, and godly and moral character.

Learn healthy communication, conflict resolution, social, and relationship skills; teach and practice these skills consistently with your children.

Ask your children questions and learn the image of God in them. This will also enable you to know what they are thinking, how they are believing, how they are developing in their relationship and perception of God, and where they need further development. Keep communication doors open so they will feel open to asking you about God and asking you the hard and challenging questions about life; this will also draw them to running to you for guidance rather than the world, ungodly friends, or holding things in that they should be sharing and processing with you.

Learn to recognize teachable moments and opportunities to teach your child about God, the things of God, and the world. Tailor make your revelations to their age and learning style so they can receive an eternal impartation of what you are sharing.

Allow yourself to be vulnerable with your children. Share your failures and successes and even allow your children to see you repentant, challenged, and pursuing trust, confidence, guidance, purpose in the Lord so they can learn from your life; This also gives them a realistic role model of what it means to walk with the Lord in a covenant lifestyle.

Take time to celebrate breakthroughs, promises and prophecies coming to pass, destiny moments, goals accelerations and milestones. Have times of thanksgiving and worship with your children of what God has done and take time to feast and celebrate his goodness. Teach them how to joy in God so they will know him in all his glory – in all of his goodness – in the fullness of sonship.

Writing Child Destiny Plans with God

Spend time asking God about the seed that is in your womb. Ask him who each child is and what their purpose is in the earth. Journal what he shares.

If your child is already born, spend time hearing God concerning their destiny and life's vision. Journal what he shares.

Keep a journal of all the prophecies, promises, and revelation God releases to you about you children. Be sure to journal the dates they were given, times they were given, and what God spoke. This can be given to your child later in life so that you they will know God's heart for them has followed them their entire life.

Be careful who you allow to be around your child and who you let speak and impart into their lives. Be quick to break the powers of any words spoken over your child that are contrary to what God has revealed. This includes teachers, ministers, prophets, strangers, family members, friends, peers. If it is not the word of the Lord, rebuke it off your child's life, and decree what God says over them.

Teach your child how to discern ungodly and unhealthy words that are contrary to God's plan for their lives and teach them how to break the power of these words off their lives.

Build your child up in God confidence by asking God what is the standard, character, nature, they need to sustain in destiny and what their remnant and purpose is in the earth. Cultivate them in that, so that they will not allow people to speak or treat them any less that what God is declaring for their lives.

Spend time asking God for strategy for how to education, train, equip, develop, and cultivate your child in their destiny and life's vision.

Spend consistent time educating, training, and praying with you child concerning what God says, and declaring his truth over them.

Break off anyway your child's identity has already been cultivated contrary to the identity of God.

Learn your generational curses, cycles, patterns, and propensities, and that of your mate; spend time consistently breaking these curses and putting familiar spirits out of your family line.

Take a stand with your child with learning godly behaviors and patterns and living through them, so you all can break the powers and close gateways to generational cycle, patterns, and propensities.

Seek God for the destiny killing spirits that will try to thwart your child's purpose and calling. Destiny killing spirits tend to track children throughout life in effort to delay or stifle their purpose. When the child overcomes one situation and you think that spirit is overthrown, a similar situation may show up in another area of their lives where they are combating those same spirits. This is because destiny killing spirit operate through a demonic system so these spirits will show up at church, school, the community. It is a system of familiar spirits that have collaborated to thwart your child's destiny.

Learn your authority over demonic spirits and teaching your children their authority over them. Train your child in warfare according to the calling and office that is on their lives. Never think they are too young to combat big demons. David was but a youth when he fought Goliath. Your child is equipped with grace and power to slay the demons that would come for their lives.

Be watchful of your child's play, the dreams they say they are experiencing, and who you allow them to hang around. Do not allow them to play with imaginary friends that could be familiar spirits. You will know that they are familiar spirits if they constantly talk about them, wait on them to visit, can explain what they look like or have on, only want to play with this spirit; as familiar spirits seeks to isolate children and have them dependent on them rather than real relationships. Cast these spirits out you house and let children know these are demons and is not their imagination at work. Deal with all nightmare demons that attack your child in their sleep. If children are speaking of spirits hiding in closets and under beds, do not take these comments lightly. Pray over their room and command these spirits to go. Teach them how to cast these spirits out when they try to be part of their lives. Protect your child's innocence by not allowing them to hang out with just anyone or stay over everyone's house, even family members. Familiar molesting and rape spirits are always seeking out children so that can steal their purity and strip them of their God identity.

As your child would participate in church, school, and community activities, be mindful of what the true purpose of their calling is and make sure they are reaching their ordained remnant and impacting the earth by God's design.

Teach your child about God and how to have a covenant relationship with him so that they can hear God regarding their destiny and calling for themselves.

Know that as your child grows, the strategies and revelations for cultivating destiny will change to accommodate them evolving in their God identity. Therefore, do not put God in a box regarding your child. Seek him regularly – in and out of season – concerning who your child is and who they are becoming so he can provide you with the tools you need to cultivate them in destiny.

DECREEING DESTINY SUCCESS TO YOU AND YOUR CHILD!

Shift!

Helping Children Cope with Destiny

As adults, we know that going through life can teach us that there are certain trials and warfare are part of the process of refining and standing in our calling as God's chosen people. Noted below are common scriptures that believers use to remind ourselves of our identity and authority in Christ when we face fiery trials:

Jeremiah 1:5 New International Bible Before I formed you in the womb I knew you, before you were born I set you apart; I appointed you as a prophet to the nations.

Psalm 139:13 New International Bible For you created my inmost being; you knit me together in my mother's womb.

Consider, if there are times when adults, who personally know God, struggle to operate in their identity and authority, how much more of an internal struggle may children face being chosen for something they do not fully understand. There are so many factors that young people must naturally manage that throwing in a spiritual calling from a God, whom they may not know, can completely overwhelm them or turn them away from God.

Common struggles that children chosen from the womb may grapple with include peer pressure, their identity, feeling safe and important, negotiating relationships, time management, generational curses, typical physical and cognitive growth, and juggling society's audacious stand against God with pressure to choose God over a glamorized world. The truth is that when a child is chosen from birth it can become another weight to that child's life if they are not equipped from a young age to walk in destiny. Teaching children that they are waiting for their destiny can make God seem like a task master who is waiting for them to get everything right to release good things for them and that is not the kind of God we serve.

There are several things we should considered when we want to help a child cope with being chosen from the womb. Those are,

- Warfare
- Weariness
- modeling.

Merriam-Webster online dictionary defines warfare as *"an earnest effort for superiority or victory over another. In relation to our discussion, warfare would be a child's earnest effort for victory over the enemy."* It is important that a child does not see victory and their destiny as passive experiences, but things that come through prayer, knowing and activating God's word, and lovingly obeying the Father. These are strategies that are important to be actively taught and practically applied in a child's daily life. As seen through historical genocide, recent school shootings, sexual trafficking, and perversion of child identity there is a demonic assignment against children from the womb. When helping children cope with being chosen, it is important that we teach them who God says they are, but it is just as important to ask for their spiritual eyes to be opened so they can see the warfare aspect of their life. When they have knowledge, they can better understand when things go awry or they struggle with things naturally, emotionally, or spiritually. The goal is not to scare the child but to build their confidence in knowing that there are more with us, in God's kingdom, than on the other side.

2Kings 6:17 New International Bible And Elisha prayed, "Open his eyes, LORD, so that he may see." Then the LORD opened the servant's eyes, and he looked and saw the hills full of horses and chariots of fire all around Elisha.

When a child can understand that God loves them, has a powerful kingdom, and has sent his angels to protect and help them navigate their current life situations it reveals God to be more than an adult God, a myth, or tradition and thus makes him accessible to them. If we are too afraid to expose children early to the invisible kingdom they will not be prepared and aware of their surroundings. However, when a child is exposed to the truth of God it gives them a spiritual arsenal that will equip them to deal with their struggles. It is not a parent's job to save their child. That is God's business. A parent's job is to expose their child to who God is, what he says, and who they go against.

One practical way for parents to help children cope with being called is to fill their Spirit with the Word so that when they face struggles and temptations, the Holy Spirit can remind them as they walk out their daily lives.

John 14:26 New International Bible says "But the Advocate, the Holy Spirit, whom the Father will send in my name, will teach you all things and will remind you of everything I have said to you."

A second way to help children cope with being called from the womb is to put **Deuteronomy 11:17-20** into action at home. God made it very plain that he wanted parents to expose their children to his word at home. This scripture instructs parents to make it easy to talk about God, their issues, and practical ways to work through issues using God's word. When we follow God's plan for teaching our children from the womb, it makes room for God to prove himself to them.

Deuteronomy 11:17-20 New International Bible says, You shall therefore impress these words of mine on your heart and on your soul; and you shall bind them as a sign on your hand, and they shall be as frontals on your forehead. "You shall teach them to your sons, talking of them when you sit in your house and when you walk along the road and when you lie down and when you rise up. "You shall write them on the doorposts of your house and on your gates.

Ideas for activating *Deuteronomy 11:17-20* at home include:
- Sharing bible stories and/or scriptures that speak about God's angels fighting for God's people
- Teaching scripture affirmations that speak about God's invisible kingdom or love for his people
- Having candid conversations about a child's struggles and working together to find scriptures to apply or for comfort. This models for them how to do search God's word or his heart on their own.
- Helping children create a prayer journal to write their concerns, struggles, and praise reports so they can look

back at how God has kept them and will continue to meet them when they seek him.

When children understand that God wants to reveal who he is to them it creates a hunger to learn more about him. This understanding also helps reduce the weariness that many Christian children face when being raised in church. Many children engage in life and activities through a church culture or routine, but they do not know God's kingdom so they get weary doing the religious activities since they feel it will not apply to them until later.

Merriam-Webster online dictionary defines weariness as, "*the state of being bored.*" Many children feel bored when talking about God because they do not think they can relate to someone they cannot see or don't feel good enough to get good things from God. Hence a huge goal to helping a child cope with being called from the womb is to make God relevant to them on their level. Avoiding temptation at all costs or pushing our children to be a perfect Christian should not be the goal because sin is a real part of the world, we all live in.

1Corinthians 10:13 New International Bible No temptation has overtaken you except what is common to mankind. And God is faithful; he will not let you be tempted beyond what you can bear. But when you are tempted, he will also provide a way out so that you can endure it.

We are all tempted and so will our children be, so we need to equip them to face the sin set before them. However, when someone knows God, the world loses its glamor in relation to knowing the King. Thus, the goal as parents in helping our children cope is to open doors for God to reveal himself to them using open conversations, acts of service, transparency from our journey, and allowing them to be imperfect as they learn who Christ is to them. When parents show children that God is a caring God who loves them, even in their flaws, and wants the best for them he will work in their heart to help them cope with being called by him.

Romans 2:4 New Living Bible Don't you see how wonderfully kind, tolerant, and patient God is with you? Does this mean nothing to you? Can't you see that his kindness is intended to turn you from your sin?

Another matter that is important in helping children cope with being called from the womb is modeling a true Christian journey. It is not always pretty but it is victorious so children should see parents being transparent on their own journey. While children do not need to know everything that happens in a parents' life, it can be helpful for them to see someone model and then help them work through their struggles using God's word. If a lifestyle that is presented to children by their parents is consistent, aligned with the word, nonjudgmental, and consistently bearing fruit of the Spirit children will desire to follow their parents' footsteps to get the same positive results. This last component is putting the law of sowing found in Galatians into effect.

Galatians 6:7 New Living Translation "*Don't be misled—you cannot mock the justice of God. You will always harvest what you plant*"

Before completing this chapter, it is important to note that while it is important to reveal God through his word, it is a parent's fruit that will become their child's expectation for living in Christ. Therefore, modeling a genuine relationship and godly character is imperative to showing children how to cope with being called from the womb. There are several examples in the bible of how parents sowed into their child and the result of how child comfortable their child felt living for God at a young age. Let's explore two examples. One being a positive outcome and another being a negative outcome.

Hannah and Samuel

Hannah had a son named Samuel. He grew up to be a respected prophet of God, but in his childhood his mother was a praying woman who did her duties as a mom and wife, was a consistent example of living for God, and placed her son in an environment to serve and personally experience God. While Hannah allowed Samuel to use his gifts to serve in the temple as a child, Hannah would encourage him by making him little robes and bringing them to him as he served God. Her consistent character and positioning him to experience God on his level allowed Samuel to see God move early in his life and led to him continuing to grow in the Lord throughout his youth to adulthood.

Isaac and Jacob

When Isaac's wife was pregnant with their sons, the Lord told Isaac that his sons would become nations and that the nation from Jacob would be served by his brother's lineage. Throughout Jacob's life he struggled with being deceptive. Although Jacob had a calling on his life from the womb, he struggled with deceit throughout this life. In fact, his father used deception to serve his family when Jacob was a boy. Jacob did not have a consistent example of godly fruit in front of him as his father was deceptive in Gerar to protect his family and his mother instructed him to use trickery to get a blessing. This lack of consistency in modeling godly character from his parents did not help in Jacob's own struggle with deceit and being called from the womb. Therefore, Jacob continued to struggle with deceit while caused him difficulties in his life. He had to flee from his family, experienced fear, and struggled with God and man because he was not properly equipped with how to cope with being called from the womb.

These examples further indicate the importance of equipping our children to deal with weariness and warfare while modeling consistent character on our own journey with Christ so that our child desires to follow Christ at an early age. Children will face temptation and natural struggles of life, but when exposed to personal experiences with God it creates a door that God can walk through to introduce himself personally to our children. It is then that, like Samuel, our children will grow up in the presence of the Lord and be taught of the Holy Spirit how they should walk.

Helping Children Cope with Stressors

When something is ranked number two, it is typically viewed with great importance or significance; but what happens when suicide is now the number two reason for death among young people? According to the Center for Disease Control and Prevention, suicide is the 2nd leading cause of death for ages 10-34. Although believers would like to believe their child is immune, these statistics include children believers as well.

Ecclesiastes 9:11 New International Bible says, *"I have seen something else under the sun: The race is not to the swift or the battle to the strong, nor does food come to the wise or wealth to the brilliant or favor to the learned; but time and chance happen to them all."*

Time and chance happen to everyone, including children, but many times young people struggle with handling the stress of life in a way that would agree with God. Common stressors that young people of all ages face are fear of the unknown or the future, handling their time, being accepted, and managing family stressors. While working through their own stressful moments, it is also important to know that there are many competing voices in our society that have been sent to influence how young people conduct themselves. These competing voices do not always align with God's word and may include social media, internet, television programming, ungodly teachers or adults, changing family institutions, shifting political agendas, and even religious agendas. These voices can get so loud that young people get confused and overwhelmed to the point of taking their own lives or walking away from doing things in agreement with God.

Just like children in our society, competing voices or cultures were a frequent issue for the children of Israel. God's consistent message to his children were for them to remain holy or separate and this instruction remains the same for young and older believers today. In an unholy world, being separate as the chosen people of God can be intimidating to a child or teen. However, there was one strategy that God consistently used to help his people work through the stressors they faced- mentorship. Mentorship is an experienced or trusted advisor helping someone that is still learning a skill, mindset, or expectation. As young people go through their struggles it can feel as if they are inadequate or unequipped to handle situations in a godly manner.

Mentorship creates an environment where an older person helps a younger person overcome their struggles, answer questions, and offers practical tools for the young person to grow into who they were created to be. Mentorship is particularly helpful for teens and tweens, as psychology shares that parents are no longer the significant voice in their child's life during those stages of development. Nevertheless, parents, coaches, youth workers, teachers, trusted family members, or pastors are all great options for a trusted mentor for a young person if there is a mutual goal established between the young person and mentor. Parents and adults adopting a mentoring mindset is one of the most powerful strategies in leading and keeping a young person to Christ. Components of effective mentorship, which can be used at any age, include active listening, non-judgmental communication, open dialogue, and a partnership mentality. Many times, we indoctrinate children into Christianity; however, mentorship was the consistent model in the bible to help young people learn and grow in their journey with Christ. Let's review several successful mentoring relationships that led to young people knowing Christ and overcoming bad choices or difficult situations.

Moses and Joshua

Joshua was called to be a leader but faced challenges of conquering a land that was full of opposition. Today, we may call this stressor bullies, negativity, or the odds stacked against a child. Moses taught and mentored Joshua in his calling. In *Exodus 24:13-14*, Moses took Joshua up into the mountain with him so he could learn how to seek God and face his stressors or challenges as a leader. Joshua went on to be Moses' successor and a great leader for Israel based on what he was taught by his mentor.

Elijah and Elisha

In *2Kings 2*, Elisha was going to be left alone to use his gift of prophecy. In today's society we may call this stress grief, abandonment, or fear. Nevertheless, Elijah was a great mentor who taught and showed Elisha how to operate in his miracle mantle, so he could personally know God, experience God, and not be alone. Elisha kept asking questions before Elijah was taken to heaven, as he gleaned from the anointing that was on his life. Elijah followed God's plan to reveal divine strategies to Elisha for operating as a prophet of God. Elisha was able to work double the miracles because of what was imparted into him through his mentor Elijah.

Jesus and Disciples

Matthew 4-28 accounts for how Jesus' disciples faced many stressors on their three-year journey with Christ. They faced the equivalent to today's gossip, negativity, complaints, criticism, persecution, fear, insecurity, and character flaws. Even through all these stressors, Jesus listened to and answered their questions, gave them opportunities to experience the power of God, chastised, taught, communed, and prayed for the disciples. This enabled them to mature in the gospel and in destiny.

Samuel and David

In *1Samuel 16*, Samuel anointed David as a teenager to be King, but he went on to become a part of his journey and success as the King of Israel. David had a heart after God but also faced stressors such as conceiving a baby out of wedlock, murdering someone, and stealing someone's wife. Yet, Samuel was intricate in giving David encouragement, teaching him biblical principles, confronting him during bad choices, and praying for him.

These are just several examples of the power of biblical mentoring. When young people face challenges - whether natural or spiritual - having a trusted adult to listen and help has proven to be invaluable in young people handling the stressors of life. There is one additional key component of helping young people deal with stress that can also be seen in the examples. Offering practical strategies to the stressors young people are facing is a powerful tool that helps provide aid to their situation, as well as an understanding that God will be their present help in the time.

Psalm 46:1 New International Bible God is our refuge and strength, an ever-present help in trouble.

God's goal is always that young people will know that he is God. God used the bible to show that he will send seasoned believers to lead young believers to Christ where they covenant with him in a destiny lifestyle. These seasoned believers lead through the art of accountability, active listening, role modeling, and strategy. It is also important that we use similar strategies to equip our young people in God's Kingdom with trusted leaders to help them find their way.

Charge to Teachers

American children spend on average about a thousand hours at school each year. This does not include after school programs or extracurricular activities. A SHIFT must take place in teachers realizing that they do more than just teach children regarding educational subject matters or encourage and empowering children regarding day to day issues. Teachers must comprehend that are vital to children learning their identity and SHIFTING into destiny as a lifestyle. For teachers are the secondary covering to children being adequately trained and equipped in who they are to become in the earth.

Biblically the role of a teacher is identified as a spiritual office.

Ephesians 4:9-13 The Amplified Bible contends: (What does "he ascended" mean except that he also descended to the lower, earthly regions? He who descended is the very one who ascended higher than all the heavens, in order to fill the whole universe.) So Christ himself gave the apostles, the prophets, the evangelists, the pastors and teachers, to equip his people for works of service, so that the body of Christ may be built up until we all reach unity in the faith and in the knowledge of the Son of God and become mature, attaining to the whole measure of the fullness of Christ.

The Ephesians 4 mandate is to:
- ✓ Equip
- ✓ Build in faithful unity and knowledge

✓ Bring maturity and the fullness such that God's children are no longer subject to deception by crafty demonic schemes

❖ Teachers are change agents. Teachers possess the power to govern and impact a child's destiny comparable to a parent.

❖ Teachers can either empower or disenfranchise the child's destiny. As teachers instill knowledge that trains and equips a child for their future.

❖ Teachers helps to identify, pull out, and cultivate the child's gifts. talents. potential, skill sets, and intellectual capacity.

❖ Teachers can determine if a child is held back or SHIFTED forward.

❖ Teachers either awakens and highlights a child's learning style or stifles it.

❖ Teachers can be the catalyst for whether that child loves learning, loves their identity, or dreads learning and dreads who they are in the earth.

❖ Teachers are either a protector of that child and their destiny, or an opponent who exploits and exposes that child to the enemy or perpetrators.

❖ TEACHERS ARE TRUTH BEARERS. They do not teach their opinions, but God's facts ad analysis. They impart knowledge and skills to encourage, empower, and direct their child in living a Christ-like life, through the blueprint of God that is upon that child. They legislate authority by overseeing the educational and training capacities regarding what they are teaching, including writing and developing curriculum and performing teaching and training duties in accordance to what the children in their jurisdiction needs.

Titus 2:7-8 New Living Bible And you yourself must be an example to them by doing good works of every kind. Let everything you do reflect the integrity and seriousness of your teaching. Teach the truth so that your teaching can't be criticized. Then those who oppose us will be ashamed and have nothing bad to say about us.

To be effective, the teacher must apply the instruction to their own lives and be an example of the truth. As they emulate the truth, their teaching cannot be criticized. Impartation occurs because they sow the revelation to which they carry, into their students.

It is important for parents to know who is teaching their children and what their belief systems are. Asking essential questions is key to making sure your child is being provided the greatest educational opportunities possible, and that the teacher is being exactly who they need to be to your child and their future. This is also vital to dismantling any witchcraft and idolatrous practices a teacher may use with your child. For many teachers do not carrying the truth of God. They are blatant witches who intentionally infiltrate the school system to demonically influence children or ignorantly engage in these practices because they deem them healthy learning or behavioral modification methods.

Psalms 32:8 The Amplified Bible I will instruct you and teach you in the way you should go; I will counsel you [who are willing to learn] with My eye upon you.
Exodus 18:20 The Amplified Bible You shall teach them the decrees and laws. You shall show them the way they are to live and the work they are to do.

1Thessalonians 4:1-2 The Amplified Bible Finally, believers, we ask and admonish you in the Lord Jesus, that you follow the instruction that you received from us about how you ought to walk and please God (just as you are actually doing) and that you excel even more and more [pursuing a life of purpose and living in a way that expresses gratitude to God for your salvation]. For you know what commandments and precepts we gave you by the authority of the Lord Jesus.

Parents must also listen to teachers when they providing feedback concerning behavioral, peer, and learning issues. Teachers should not be viewed as the enemy. What they say should be taken into consideration as such information can be vital to the progress a child can make if these issues are unchallenged in their character, relationship interactions, and educational processing.

Teachers should provide instruction that show children the way in which they are to go in character, identity, destiny, progress, evolution, and success. As they help children identify their gifts and callings, their teaching brings encouragement and empowerment to ensure children progress on their course with God.

Teachers contend against demonic powers and vain imaginations that attempt to exalt themselves against the knowledge and kingdom of God in a child's life and destiny. They correct, rebuke, convict, and expose ungodly truths, error, mixture, flightiness, falsehoods, counterfeits, haughty, and foolish wisdom. Their main purpose is to keep children from being destroyed through faulty, prideful, wicked doctrines, systems, and imaginations.

1Corinthians 1:27 *But God hath chosen the foolish things of the world to confound the wise; and God hath chosen the weak things of the world to confound the things which are mighty.*

Proverbs 16:18 *Pride goeth before destruction, and an haughty spirit before a fall.*

2Corinthians 10:4-5 *(For the weapons of our warfare are not carnal, but mighty through God to the pulling down of strong holds;) Casting down imaginations, and every high thing that exalteth itself against the knowledge of God, and bringing into captivity every thought to the obedience of Christ; And having in a readiness to revenge all disobedience, when your obedience is fulfilled.*

Romans 8:37-39 *Nay, in all these things we are more than conquerors through him that loved us. For I am persuaded, that neither death, nor life, nor angels, nor principalities, nor powers, nor things present, nor things to come, Nor height, nor depth, nor any other creature, shall be able to separate us from the love of God, which is in Christ Jesus our Lord. Powers are high ranking supernatural demons or demonic influences that cause evil and sin in the world.*

Powers are those who operate in positions of influence much like teachers, to control, possess, confuse, sway, and transform the minds, beliefs, and standards of people, especially children - the younger generation. Powers seek to implement alternative doctrines and educational discourses that are self-focused, people focused, or demonic focused. Their mandate is idolatry – exchanging the worship of the creature for creation.

Romans 1:22-26 Professing themselves to be wise, they became fools, And changed the glory of the uncorruptible God into an image made like to corruptible man, and to birds, and fourfooted beasts, and creeping things. Wherefore God also gave them up to uncleanness through the lusts of their own hearts, to dishonour their own bodies between themselves: Who changed the truth of God into a lie, and worshipped and served the creature more than the Creator, who is blessed for ever. Amen. For this cause God gave them up unto vile affections: for even their women did change the natural use into that which is against nature.

Powers engage in this demonic authority through the legislation of demonic teachings, misguided inferences, demonic teachings, misguided inferences, opinions, explorations, impressions, and considerations, culture trends, enactment demonic policies and laws that appear to be good and what is best for people, lands, or regions, yet separate and sway them from the will, plans, purposes, and standards of God. Teaching officers cast these powers down. Teaching officers contend against powers in warfare, intercession, instruction, proclamation, scribing curriculum, while sounding the alarm in communities and systems, thus providing education in the truths and ways of God.

Like Jesus, who often taught rather than preached and was known as a teacher, heavenly signs and wonders should follow teaching officers. They have the power through their instruction to SHIFT darkness out and light in - to SHIFT the kingdom of the devil out and the kingdom of God in.

Teachers can pray over their classroom such that the kingdom of God reigns.

Teachers can anoint their hands and every time they encounter students, they can touch them with the officiating government of the instruction, character, nature, presence, purpose, of heaven.

Teachers can seek God for curriculum that transforms lives and nurture destinies.

Teachers can seek God regarding the learning style of students, and rather than putting them in special needs classes or alternative schools, or suggesting they be prescribed medications, they can meet that child in their unique blueprint, and help cultivate greatness in them.

Teachers can command demons to come out of children rather than allowing them to run the classroom, bully other students, and be a disruption to them being able to teach successfully and joyfully.

Teachers can walk in a divine knowing and discernment to perceive the issues that child is going through at home and become an intervention of protection and guard against their purity, innocence, emotional and physical wellness, and destiny.

If teachers went to work every day with this mindset, destinies of children would be cultivated and evolve as a norm in our society. I CHARGE teachers to SHIFT into their God given office as gatekeepers of children and their ordained purpose in the earth. You are more than just an educator. You are a legislator of the kingdom of God. Decreeing you officiate properly from this day forth in Jesus name. **SHIFT RIGHT NOW! SHIFT!**

Resources

Books by Taquetta Baker
Sustaining the Vision Workbook
The Great Awakening: Igniting Regional Revival

Online Reference Sources
Abort73.com
Annboroch.com/category/vaccines/
Blueletterbible.com
Biblestudytools.com
Childhelp.org
Dictionary.com
Forbes.com/sites/johnfarrell/2018/04/19/tracing-consciousness-in-the-brains-of-infants/#7b976165722f
International Labour Organization
Olivetree.com
Sciencedirect.com/science/article/abs/pii/0163638386900251
Strong's Exhaustive Bible Concordance Online Bible Study Tools
Thinktwice.com
Vaccine.guide

Photography and Editorial Team
Cover photo vision by Tashema Davis, Owner of Echo Gallery

Editorial Team:
Amanda Latrice, Nina Cook, and Dr. Kathy Williams

> *You can link with me or any of my support team through Facebook.*
> *Connecting with me will give you access to each one on the team.*

Books Shannon Has Published
I Am What God Says I Am (ages 3-10)

Tough Stuff (ages 11-17)

The Ex Factor (ages 18+)

Kingdom Shifters Books & Apparel
Available at Kingdomshifters.com and Amazon.com

BOOKS FOR EVERYONE

Healing The Wounded Leader

Kingdom Shifters Decree That Thang

There Is An App For That

Kingdom Watchman Builder On The Wall

Embodiment Of A Kingdom Watchman

Dismantling Homosexuality Handbook

Kingdom Heirs Decree That Thang

Birthing Books That Shift Generations

Fivefold Operations Volume I, II, III

Unmasking The Power Of The Scouts

Kingdom Keys To Governing Relationships

Let There Be Sight

Atmosphere Changers

Apostolic Governing

Apostolic Mantle

Dance From Heaven To Earth

Annihilating Church Hurt

Feasting In His Presence

Prayers That Shift Atmospheres

Releasing The Vision

Discerning The Voice Of God

BOOKS FOR DANCERS
Dancers! Dancers! Dancers! Decree That Thang

Spirits That Attack Dance Ministers & Ministries

Dance & Fivefold Ministry

Dance from Heaven to Earth

CD'S
Decree That Thang CD

Kingdom Heirs Decree That Thang CD

Teaching & Worship CD's

www.ingramcontent.com/pod-product-compliance
Lightning Source LLC
Chambersburg PA
CBHW051825040426
42447CB00006B/377